IN
THE
RING
OF
THE
RISE

IN THE RING OF THE RISE

by Vincent C. Marinaro

illustrated by Pearce Bates

CROWN PUBLISHERS, INC.

NEW YORK

Books by Vincent C. Marinaro

A MODERN DRY-FLY CODE
IN THE RING OF THE RISE

Designed by Ruth Kolbert Smerechniak

Portions of this book originally appeared in the following magazines: "The Hidden Hatch" (*Outdoor Life*, July 1969); "Big Fly: Big Trout" (*Outdoor Life*, March 1967); "Small Fly: Big Fish" (*True*, September 1972, under the title "Small Flies for Fall Fish"); "The Au Sable" (*the fly fisher*, No. 1, No. 2, 1970); "In the Ring of the Rise" (*Sports Afield*, June 1975); "A Tale of Two Waters" (*Outdoor Life*, April 1976). The model of "Felix" in Chapter 2, design courtesy of The Meyercord Co.

Library of Congress Cataloging in Publication Data

Marinaro, Vincent.
   In the ring of the rise.

   1. Trout fishing.   2. fly fishing.   I. Title.
SH687.M297 1976   799.1'7'55   76-7356
ISBN 0-517-52550-X
ISBN 0-517-52586-0 (lim. ed.)

Contents

Part One
IN THE RING OF THE RISE

1 The Anatomy of the Rise *5*
2 What the Fish Sees and Does Not See *9*
3 Fishing to the Ring of the Rise *27*
4 Rod Function: Rod Design *39*

Part Two
ADVENTURES WITH SPECIAL FLY PATTERNS

5 A Game of Nods *63*
6 The Hidden Hatch *91*
7 Big Fly: Big Trout *117*
8 Small Fly: Big Fish *131*

Part Three
TROUT RIVERS IN PROFILE

9 Anatomy of the Limestone
    and Freestone Trout Waters *147*
10 The Au Sable *165*
    INDEX *183*

Part One

IN
THE
RING
OF
THE
RISE

". . . the tyrannical fascination which angling holds for all those who have once been initiated into its mysteries.

"The riddles it presents are endless; as fast as one is resolved, or appears to be resolved, by the pertinacious and thoughtful, another confronts him challengingly and engages his efforts. Sometimes the solution of one riddle is in itself the creation of another. And so, this endless tyranny goes on. Only those become weary of angling who bring nothing to it but the idea of catching fish."

—RAFAEL SABATINI

Chapter One

The Anatomy of the Rise

A TROUT LIVES IN A SECRET WORLD. IT IS A SMALL WORLD IN WHICH many dramatic events are played out in watery obscurity, veiled from the keenest eyes. And even though he is stalked and pursued relentlessly by the most attentive land creature on earth, his life-style remains much of a mystery. Except in especially contrived circumstances, there are only faint glimpses, flashes, and rolls—brief visual hints of his presence. Rarely is there a total exposure.

A trout is vulnerable to the fisherman because he eats. That is the theme of our inquiry. It is, by far, the best avenue of penetration, and it must begin with the most important of all visual evidence—namely, the surface disturbance of the water created by a foraging trout.

The ring of the rise, often described as a riseform, is the distinctive identifying mark of a feeding trout. Other kinds of fish can make such a mark but it has more significance for the trout fisherman, and particularly for the dry-fly fisherman, than anyone else. It means also a great deal to the wet-fly and nymph fisherman. That mark can be made by subsurface feeding, too, when such feeding takes place close to the underside of the surface film. For the trout fisherman it is as important as a fingerprint or footprint in human affairs.

Unfortunately, the riseform, important as it is, does not tell the fisherman very much, certainly not as much as he needs to know. It tells him only that a trout is feeding and in a few circumstances it may tell him what kind of an insect is being taken. That is all.

The riseform does not disclose to the fisherman the trout's observation or feeding station. It does not reveal the direction from which the rise came. It does not tell how far the trout drifted with the insect before the rise occurred, or on which side of his face the trout has been feeding, or whether he took the insect facing upstream, across stream, or downstream. There are many more questions to be answered. Actually, the riseform is only the final act in what may be, many times, a very complicated process of acquiring a tiny bite of food.

A trout does not eat in the manner of humans, or even as animals do. Humans have worked out a very satisfactory way of eating. We sit in a comfortable chair before a solidly positioned table on which are displayed, within easy reach, all the food that we may need for a full meal, and we do not need to spend much time at our eating. It is usually a very relaxing and pleasant affair. We do not go rushing about the dining room for endless hours, plucking a little bite here and there, tasting some, inspecting some, eating some; sometimes spitting out some that we do not like.

A trout does all this and more. He is forever sorting out things, constantly bringing all possible food under close scrutiny; and he questions every bite that he gets. Eating, for him, is not a simple matter. His dinner table is always in motion, sometimes very fast, and heaving violently. The bits of food coming his way are moving just as fast as the table. Then there is the endless exertion to hold his place at that table. He is not allowed to remain there but must move his entire body, sometimes a distance of many feet, to obtain something from the moving table. And always, there is that recurring crisis of inspection and decision making. All this is usually concluded by an amazing skill displayed in the act of interception, gracefully executed with consummate ease and precision.

Interception is an unfamiliar word in fishing language, spoken or written: When completely understood as it is applied to the eating habit it becomes abundantly clear that it is one of the most significant aspects of trout fishing. Of all the earth's creatures, other than a few species of fish, only birds of prey and some humans have developed the act of interception to a very high degree.

Subjectively, it is very difficult to say what a trout is thinking when he inspects and selects. All discussions about selectivity are only superficial. We can only speculate on his mental processes and we must continue to depend on outward manifestations for clues to his preferences in selecting certain flies. Certainly we can examine the physical process of making selections, which is by itself a marvelous thing to see, and in that examination we may discover some wonderful secrets about a trout's behavior.

Fly-fishing has now reached a very high degree of sophistication. Over a period of five centuries many things in practice have changed; many refinements have been made. The trout has not changed. His fundamental nature is still the same, no matter where you find him. He behaves the same in freestone as in limestone waters; the same in rough as in quiet water. He inspects, drifts with the insect, and selects in rough, fast water the same way that he does in quiet water. In the rougher, faster streams he operates in a somewhat smaller space-time frame. It is only a matter of degree, not of his nature. He is still the same deadly accurate hunter in pursuit of his prey. He is a kill-artist whose hunter skills are cultivated and refined from babyhood; without them he would die. His relentless pursuit of a victim is a startling study in concentrated deadlines. His way of life is a perpetual search-and-destroy mission.

The photographic essay contained in the following pages represents an attempt to penetrate his secret world, to invade the privacy of his dining room, and to pry into his eating habits. Remember, he is vulnerable to the fisherman because he eats.

The search for food, prosaic as it may seem and recorded here in dynamic attitudes and postures, conveys more powerfully than any words the intensity of his fight for life—and, importantly, the possible solutions to some of the riddles that beset the fisherman.

There is no real need to dramatize or sentimentalize in order to create an interesting story. The stark objectivity of the trout's performance is impressive enough without rhetoric.

Nothing in taking these photographs was contrived or constructed, not even an artificial blind; only a natural blind was used. These are photographs of wild trout in a natural environment. It was not an easy thing to do.

This is the way it was in one chapter of a trout's life-span.

THE SIMPLE RISE

The simple rise is the least complicated of the riseforms made by trout and usually occurs during a major hatch when the trout is sure of the food type floating downstream. It involves a quick decision by the trout and little hesitation is present. Starting at his observation post, the trout spies the fly and begins an upward and downstream drift. At a point downstream, the trout rises to the surface to meet the fly, and it is here that he will either take or refuse it. Regardless, he now returns to his holding area.

Looking closely at the water's surface, an angler may detect the rise of a trout, evidenced by a circular ring. No other details of the rise are visible. And, except for a brief flash or shadowy movement, this is about all a fisherman will ever see of the feeding activity.

However, here is a look at what really happens when a trout strikes, in photographs taken from a natural blind where elevation and light were ideal for looking in on the private life of native trout.

"... a small world in which many dramatic events are played out in watery obscurity, veiled from the keenest eyes."

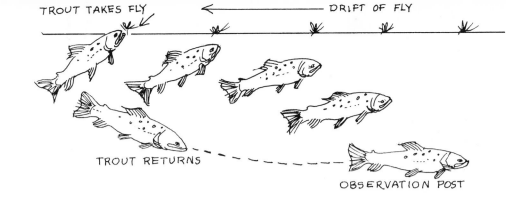

TROUT TAKES FLY ← ——————— DRIFT OF FLY

TROUT RETURNS

OBSERVATION POST

The trout is a hunter. In this photograph the trout is at his feeding station, lying in wait, watching as his dinner table passes overhead. There is an alert look about him as he is waiting, easily fanning the current to hold his position. He then begins a simple rise, which is a vertical and backward movement that will place him below or downstream so he will be able to intercept the insect. Note particularly the flow of weeds below the trout. This is always from right to left with the flow of current in these photographs, which will help in determining the trout's true positions as he executes the simple rise.

In this photograph he has seen something and has started his tip-up. This is always evidenced by preliminary acceleration of fins and tail to gain headway against the current. This is also the beginning of the calculations needed to complete his maneuvers or a successful interception of the insect.

Gaining elevation and drifting backward, he is narrowing the gap and homing in on his victim with deadly precision.

After the trout has reached point-blank range, he is ready to strike. Many trout feed on only one side of their face—that is, they take a fly from either the left or right on the drift. This leads to the speculation that trout may have a master eye and that they will position themselves where they can best see and then take a drifting insect.

This is the end of the strike and the beginning of the surface riseform. This is also the early stage of the riseform, which is roughly triangular or wedge-shaped, not easily seen by the naked eye.

Here you can see the rise and the progression of the riseform to a circular shape. The push of the current against the apex of the wedge will complete the circular form. The progression is lightning fast and is almost impossible to detect with the naked eye.

Most importantly, note that the riseform is always *behind* the trout. This, plus the fact that he has now drifted backward, is a source of the error in estimating the correct position of the trout after the strike. In most cases, by the time the circular rings are seen, the trout is already heading back to his observation post upstream.

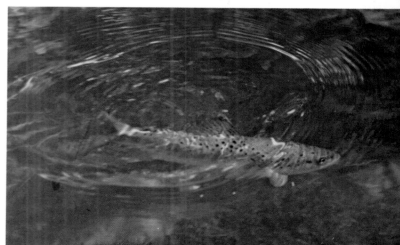

THE COMPOUND RISE

Essentially, the compound rise is a continuation of the simple rise, but it involves a much longer drift-and-inspection period. This is because there is some doubt in the trout's mind as to the edibility of the foodstuff that is floating overhead. It is important to realize here that, as opposed to the complex rise, where the trout will allow the insect to float away from him before making the decision to strike, in the compound rise the trout will stay with the insect (or artificial fly) throughout the entire drift, constantly inspecting while deciding whether to take or refuse. It is, therefore, imperative that an angler have as drag-free a float as possible.

When making a compound rise, a trout begins (as in all the other riseforms) by rising from his observation post and drifting downstream and up to view the fly. Here the fish has risen to the surface and is just about to strike.

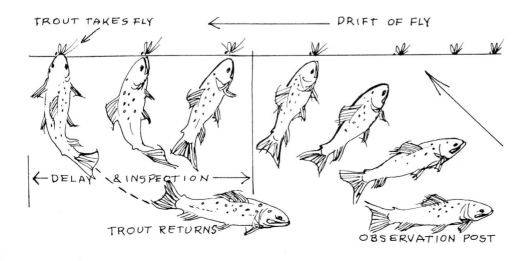

TROUT TAKES FLY ← DRIFT OF FLY

← DELAY & INSPECTION →

TROUT RETURNS

OBSERVATION POST

But for some reason, there is still too much doubt in his mind so he hesitates, swings sideways to the current, and drifts downstream with the insect. This is the beginning of a very close inspection period because he is unsure of his prey and thus must make a careful examination. Trout will do this very often with the natural as well as with the artificial fly when doubt is involved. It should be reemphasized here that due to the close inspection and long drift period associated with the compound rise, an angler's fly must be as drag-free as possible. Otherwise, the trout will usually refuse to take. The "puddle cast" is extremely useful in this situation because with it an angler can get a long drag-free drift that will be less likely to spook wary trout. I have seen fish that drifted twenty to twenty-five feet before taking; with this much time to inspect, anything unnatural will likely be detected and refused.

When the trout reaches the midway point in the drift, he will then make a final decision to strike or not. He has two options open to him at this time. He may refuse the fly, drop down and head back to his holding area, or he may take the insect, thus completing the compound rise.

THE COMPLEX RISE

The complex rise occurs when there is extreme doubt in the trout's mind as to the food-type drifting overhead. Initially, the trout rises from his holding area and begins a downstream drift, facing either upstream or across stream, delaying inspection because of his uncertainty. The rise could end here if the trout believes that it is an inedible object or if excess drag ruins an artificial's action.

At this point the trout, still very doubtful, will allow the fly, caught up in the current, to begin floating away from him. This is the time for decision. If he decides to refuse, he will return to his holding area. However, if for some reason he does decide to take (possibly the sight of the insect excites him), he will turn, facing downstream, and in a fast motion will begin pursuit. Once a trout has made the decision to chase after a fly, he will never refuse it. His mind has been made up.

At this stage of the trout's drift—when he neither accepted nor rejected the fly—the rise becomes complex because he is adding a change of direction but is hesitant about striking. This could be for reasons of color, size, rate of drift, or other factors. He is drifting with the current at the same rate as the fly.

This debating action continues and the trout starts a reverse drift to follow the insect downstream. At this time both the trout and the insect are still drifting at the same speed. Now, the trout will either choose to refuse to take and head back to his observation post, or he could choose to take it here (which would constitute a compound rise) or he could continue his drift and inspection process.

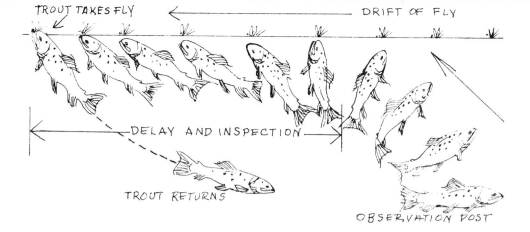

TROUT TAKES FLY ← DRIFT OF FLY

DELAY AND INSPECTION

TROUT RETURNS

OBSERVATION POST

Here the current has begun to move the insect at a faster rate than the trout's drift. At this point the trout will either refuse and go back to his holding area or he will continue his inspection as he watches the fly drift away. In this instance, the trout is leveling off and is speeding up his chase, indicating his decision to take the fly. He is determined not to lose his meal.

The speed of his chase accelerates even more now that he has chosen to take. This is evidenced by the blur in his tail movements, which cannot be stopped even with the camera's fast shutter. The trout has now abandoned all hesitancy and has but one thought in mind—to catch and devour his prey.

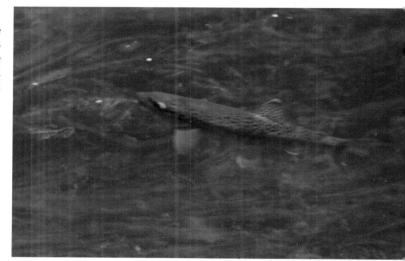

The trout has now caught up with the drifting insect and has struck. This is the reverse strike of the complex rise (hitting the fly from an upstream direction as opposed to the usual downstream strike), and it is here that we have a clue as to the reason all riseforms look alike and remain behind the trout. The most interesting thing I found out about the complex rise is that the trout never refuses the fly when he chases it downstream. He strikes, reckless of the consequences.

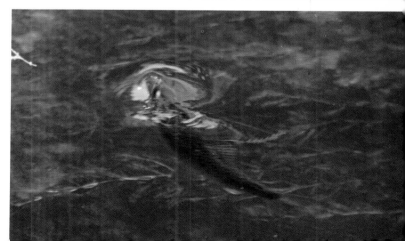

This photograph reveals the reason for the similarity of all riseforms. Immediately upon taking the insect, the fish pivots at the head and makes a tail-lashing, lightning-like swivel that carries his body around to face the current even before the riseform has begun to take shape.

This is the after-rise and completion of the circular riseform, the only part of a complicated maneuver that the average fisherman ever really sees. At this point, the trout is already on his way back to his observation post.

THE LONG DRIFT

The story connected with this photograph goes back many years to my early acquaintance with the limestoners. In the upper right background there is the ring of a rise made by a feeding trout. The rises were repeated very often in that area. When I saw them for the first time many years ago I made my approach from the left side facing the reader and made my pitches at X upstream in front of the rise. During one long summer I continued to make the same pitches to those recurring rises but I did not get a single fish. Then late in the season I approached this same area and instead of casting I went upstream, crossed over, and came down the other bank . I took a position of concealment behind the rushes at Y in the right upper background and watched closely with binoculars. In the left foreground you will notice that the main current moves from left to right until it strikes a tussock of grass in the right middleground, Z, then the current turns and heads downstream toward the rise. All the insects were being carried downstream on this current; making a right-angle turn at the tussock I discovered eventually that the trout were lying behind the tussock watching upstream toward the left entrance of the current. When the insects reached the tussock the trout left the shelter of the tussock and drifted with the insects to the position of the pictured riseform where the rise was made.

Believe it or not, those fish could not be taken unless the cast was made at C, just before the current arrived at Z and began a right-angle turn. The drift of the trout in this situation, according to my most careful estimate, was something like twenty feet!

In the several sequences shown we have seen how a trout can make many rises spread out over a considerable area as a result of the drifting and inspecting habit. Even a very good fisherman can be confused and misled by the superficial disturbances of the surface film without the knowledge of the source or direction of the strikes. A good fisherman always starts from below to cover the lowest downstream rise so as not to spook the risers above or upstream. A trout that drifted downstream ten or fifteen feet to take a fly, then hurried back to his feeding station, would not be anywhere near the lowest riseform where a good fisherman has begun to lay his casts. It would be an exercise in futility too, so there would be the same result with succeeding casts farther upstream, at least until the caster reaches the feeding station where the trout started each rise.

THE SIPPING RISE

The ultimate sophistication in fly-fishing that can be achieved is unquestionably the ability to read and interpret the different kinds of riseforms that are employed by a trout while taking surface food and subsurface food, too. It is an uncommon skill. But even when a trout is feeding close to the surface and in full view, his performance may still be perplexing and unclear to the anxiously observing fisherman.

The sipping rise is an absolutely soundless, furtive, and the most inconspicuous act in the entire catalog of a trout's eating habits. Many trout display only this particular surface riseform during their entire lives. These are the trout that live in the shadowed eddies that catch and circulate the currents in front of logjams, fallen trees, flotsam, and patches of foam. Anything carried by the currents is caught and trapped by the debris and sometimes eddied about for a very long time. In this way a great variety of insect life is paraded in front of the trout who, "lying upon a fin," can pick and choose any delectable item that suits his fancy. His eating manners are leisurely and graceful enough to arouse the admiration and envy of a Lucullus. There is nothing hurried about his inspection and selection—never any snatching or gulping. When finally he has decided to take something, this rise is quiet, deliberate, and precise. The gentle tilting upward is often so slow that the movement is almost imperceptible. The rise begins with easy undulations of the body and tail while the head elevates simultaneously with the depression of the tail. When the trout arrives within a fraction of an inch of the insect there is the bare opening of the jaws and the insect vanishes with only the faintest disturbance of the calm surface.

In front of my camera position there is a strip of duckweed extending out from the bank for a few feet. It provides a kind of cover for feeding trout. As I watched, I saw a tiny bright spot or wink of light and just behind it, close to the surface, a long, sinister-looking shape. The shape was a big trout making the sipping rise from his concealment under the duckweed. Now we shall go behind the tree to my camera position and see how it was done.

This is a big one, easing out from his cover after spotting an insect riding the current.

Beginning the uptilt with hardly any visible effort. He seems to float up toward the surface.

Closing the gap and pacing himself to meet the insect. This is the final tip-up.

The strike, done with minimal disturbance to the surface film—and there it is, that tiny wink of light that I saw from my position on the bank.

This is the most difficult of all rises to detect and many fishermen not keenly alerted to such insignificant disturbances can and often do pass by without knowing that a big fish is surface feeding.

This is the riseform that invariably accompanies the taking of tiny mayflies and minute terrestrials imprisoned in the surface film, resulting in the mysterious and very obscure flush float, scarcely known or appreciated by many fly-fishermen. Recognizing and understanding the implications contained in the sipping rise will lead to greater fly-fishing skill and the multiplication of fishing pleasure far beyond the normal mayfly season.

THE MECHANICS OF THE SWIVEL

Of all the maneuvers performed by a trout, the swivel that occurs at the conclusion of many strikes is to me the most intriguing. It takes place always when the attack is made across the current or downstream and is made primarily for the purpose of realigning his position so as to face the current and permit easier breathing. A trout hates to face away from the current.

For many years as a trout fisherman I was not fully aware of the swivel and its significance. It was not until I began to photograph feeding trout with the attendant concentration that I began to see and appreciate the swivel and its importance. It is seldom that a trout is visible before the strike is made, that results in a surface riseform. The appearance of the rise immediately draws the attention of the observing fisherman. If the light is good and the water clear, the fisherman may and oftentimes does see the trout settling down under the riseform and facing the current. But it is too late for the fisherman to see the swivel because it actually takes place before the riseform becomes visible. This is so because the swivel happens lightning fast and is made simultaneously with the opening and closing of his jaws. Any time that the swivel is part of the strike it means that the trout has made an across stream or a downstream strike, therefore misleading the fisherman as to his actual feeding position or observation post. It is entirely possible to attract a trout by pitching to the rise on a cross-stream rise but not on a downstream strike when the trout may drift many feet and mislead the fisherman into pitching to a visible rise many feet below his true feeding position or observation post. How can the fisherman overcome this difficulty? I can only suggest that if he gets no responses to his pitches that he try to see the fish or at least watch for some movement in the water that will tell him from which direction that the strike is being made. The following series of pictures depict the cross-stream strike and the accompanying swivel. It is the finest photographic sequence that I have ever made.

From his starting point or feeding station, the trout has seen something on the right side of his position and is moving across stream to launch his attack. The trout is closing in fast toward the insect.

Now its mouth has begun to open.

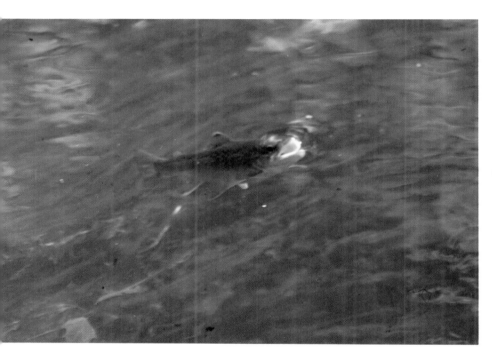

Wider.

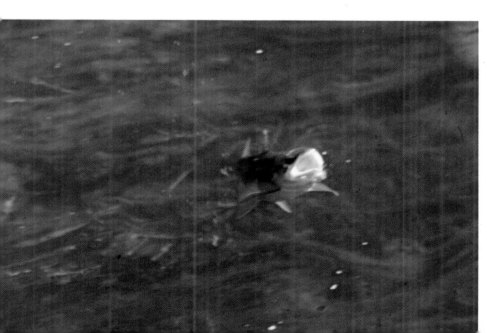

Wider! And now you are looking down into his pink gullet.

There's the strike and the beginning of that brilliant, flashing movement that aligns him with the current again and completes the same familiar riseform.

The fish's body is beginning to straighten; its head is sinking and the riseform is beginning to take shape.

Its body is much straighter now, its head deeper; the riseform is beginning to move backward.

The after-rise—and a riseform that looks just like any other riseform no matter how accomplished or from what direction.

WHAT THE TROUT SEES

This is a color photograph of the last black-and-white photograph shot through the slant tank (and shown in the next chapter). The fly at the edge of the window, where the trout sees and inspects and takes it, is drab and dull, with no distinct color rendition. Ronalds was right. Any object revealed by the low oblique rays of light is very indistinct as to color and any fine detail. This fly, viewed out of the water, had a yellow thorax, cream badger hackle, and well-marked wood-duck wings.

On the right is a freshly fallen spinner trapped in the surface film, showing the condenser effect caused by the fluting in the wings (as discussed in "A Game of Nods"). On the extreme left is the spread fiber wing, reproducing the same effect. In the center is the traditional hackle-point wing, poorly reproducing the brilliant condenser effect.

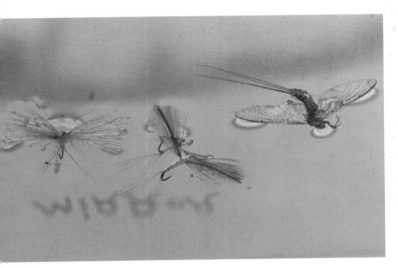

This is an entirely different result from the appearance of the dun. These are dead and dying spinners lying in the surface film. They have broken through both the window and the mirror surface film, showing them highly visible in every detail. The fine venation of the wings is perfectly discernible. But note that the wings of a spinner in the center are still in the air and very indistinct outside the window. Note the great difference in appearance from the spinner that lies with both wings flush and prone in the surface film. On the left is a Japanese beetle, amazingly well defined as to form and color—as are the spinners.

The wide-flaring, stiff-fibered wing of the successful spinner pattern.

Chapter Two

What the Fish Sees and Does Not See

FLY-FISHING IS A UNIQUE AVOCATION. IT IS INTELLECTUALLY STIMU-lating and emotionally satisfying. Its many thousands of devo-tees have the choice of occupying various levels of dedication or indulgence and remaining there, or they can climb to new heights according to the depth and width of their personal in-volvement. The peak of the fly-fisherman's ascent in terms of knowledge and appreciation is not yet in sight nor will it ever be.

There are those whose zeal and curiosity will lead them fur-

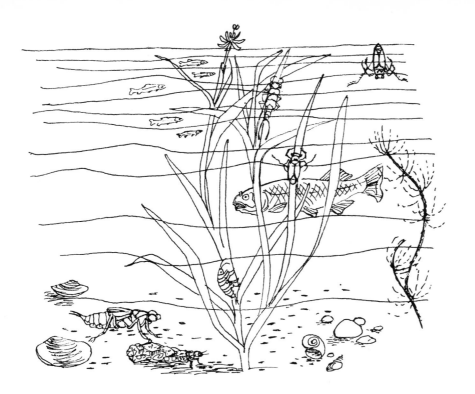

ther and further afield in an effort to penetrate the murky gloom that obscures many aspects of fly-fishing, to dredge up bits of knowledge and to pry loose a few of the delicious secrets reluctantly yielded by a grudging nature.

This chapter is offered especially to those serious students of the game who are willing to go with me deeper into the dimly lit recesses of the trout's world. This chapter need not be read at all in order to enjoy fly-fishing.

Our principal concern is connected with the laws of refraction, first significantly probed by Isaac Newton. Man's experience with refraction goes back much further than Newton, back to the dim past when the first caveman tried to spear a fish that was not actually where he saw it. We are constantly dealing with it in our daily lives; when we look through a window or our eyeglasses; when we take a picture through the lens of the camera; when we look at the stars, or when the archer tries to shoot a fish in the water. We live in a small bit of universe illuminated by light rays from our sun. Everything that we see is carried to our eyes by those light rays. Those rays travel in a straight line until they meet a denser medium such as air, water, or glass, then the ray may be bent away from a straight line and sent in a different direction, depending on the angle at which the ray strikes the denser medium. The image of any object riding the path of the light ray is also sent in a different direction with the ray no matter where it travels. The first fisherman-writer to call attention to this strange physical phenomenon was Alfred Ronalds (1802-1860), originator of a new race of angler-entomologists. His observations were very limited and affected only the view that a fish has of the angler even though he is hidden from the angler by a solid obstruction.

He pointed out correctly that a trout can see around corners just as we too can see around corners even though neither of us is aware of this. None of Ronalds's followers thought to consider that if a fish can see around corners and observe a fisherman he can also see around corners and observe the flies that come to him. Following Ronalds there were a number of famous fishermen-writers, including Frederic Halford, whose voluminous writings never once mentioned the possible effect of refraction on the view that a trout gets of the fly.

Captivated and diverted by the exquisitely drawn and colored flies (a modern obsession too!), the really important message was ignored by the dry-fly specialists and innovators of the late 1800s. If Ronalds had lived and written his book in the dry-fly era, his genius most certainly would have been exercised to include surface flies in his studies of the effects of refraction instead of being limited to the appearance of the fisherman to the fish and the fish to the fisherman.

Ronalds's remarkable book, an expensive collector's item now, is still much sought and desired. The book is scarce even though it went through at least a dozen printings, and because each printing was very small, not many of today's numerous fly-fishermen will have an opportunity to see and study it, especially the early hand-painted editions. I think, therefore, it

would be a good service to the serious student of fly-fishing to
include here a reproduction of his refraction studies, in diagram
and the applicable text, from Chapter 1 of *The Fly-Fishers Entomology*, 1836.

When Mr. A.B. (fig.1, plate 2) for instance, situated upon a
certain eminence at a given distance from a fish, C, which is near
the bottom of the water, looks over the edge of a bank, D, in the
direction AFZ, he might (if unacquainted with the laws of refraction) imagine, that neither the fish C, nor any other fish below
the line of his direct vision, AFZ, could see him; whereas C
could see AB by means of the pencil of light, AFCEB, bent, or
refracted at the surface of the water, EF, and the image of AB
would appear in the eye of the fish shortened and transferred to
GH. The fish, in fact, could see the whole of the man, round, or
over the corner of the bank, by the aid of the water above C, if
both were situated as respectively represented in the diagram;
but if the surface of the water should be at IK (i.e.) about as low
as the fish's eye, then he could not see any part of the figure AB,
because a straight or unrefracted pencil of light, ACB, would be
obstructed by the bank.

Increased obliquity in pencils of light falling from an object
upon a surface of water, is accompanied by still more rapidly increasing refraction: but the distinctness with which the object is
seen decreases in an inverse proportion.

The bending or refraction which a pencil of light, as NEOFM
(fig.2), falling very obliquely upon the surface of the water, un-
dergoes before arriving at the eye of the fish, at O, is sufficient
to produce very great indistinctness and distortion of the image
of MP formed in his eye.

But long before a pencil of light as NEL, becomes horizontal, it will not enter the water at all; consequently, although the
fish at O may see the upper part of the man situated at MP, he
will do so very indistinctly, and in a new position, because the
pencil NEOFM will be very much refracted; he will not see the
part, NL, of the man at all, because the pencil, NEL, does not
enter the water at all; and he will see probably his legs, LP (in
the clear water) because there is neither refraction nor obstruction
to prevent him. So that the figure MP will, in the eye of the fish,

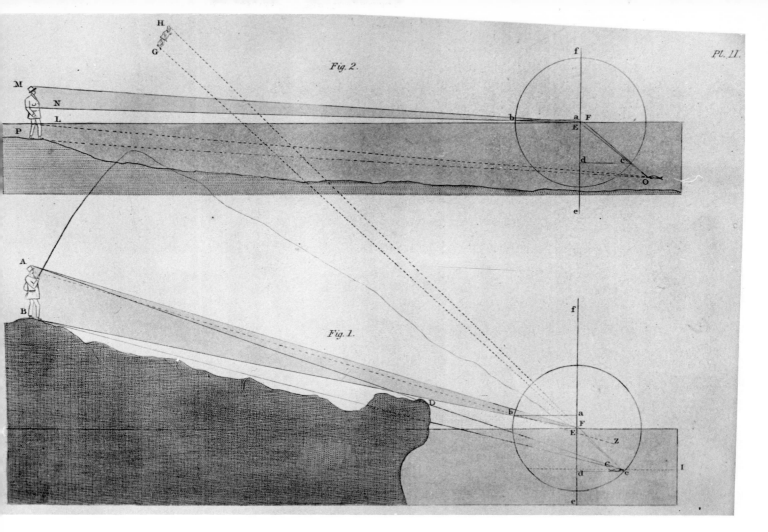

Fig. 2.

Fig. 1.

be cut into two portions, separated from each other by a long unsubstantial interval.*

The application of those two little theorems to the use of the fisherman is very obvious.

In the first place, a low bank, almost on a level with the water, is a great advantage to the fisher, who is there seen with less distinctness by his game: thus the shelving gravel beds which reach far into the Dove, and other Trout streams, are so many most advantageous positions for the angler. (PL.I.K.)

*This diagram is constructed on two well-known optical laws, viz. first, the sine a.b. of the angle of incidence, A E f, of a ray of light passing out of air into water, is always to the sine, c d, of the angle of refraction, C E e, as about four to three; and second, light will not pass out of air into water, if the angle of incidence, N E f (fig.2) exceeds 88 degrees, but will be reflected.

The old experiment of the shilling and the basin of water affords an easy practical demonstration of the first theorem in the text.

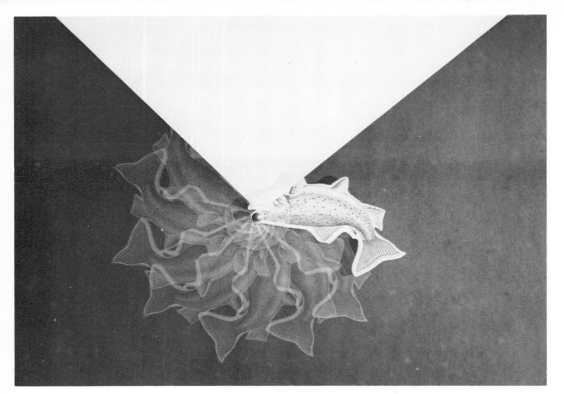

This is Felix, a very active fellow. But no matter how much he whirls and flops about, as he is doing here, he cannot change the attitude of his window. It is always poised vertically above the fish and stays with him wherever he goes. He cannot tilt the window. The sides of the inverted cone remain equal in length everywhere around the perimeter. All this is determined by the behavior of the numerous diffused light rays coming in from everywhere to form countless numbers of inverted cones of all sizes anywhere in the water.

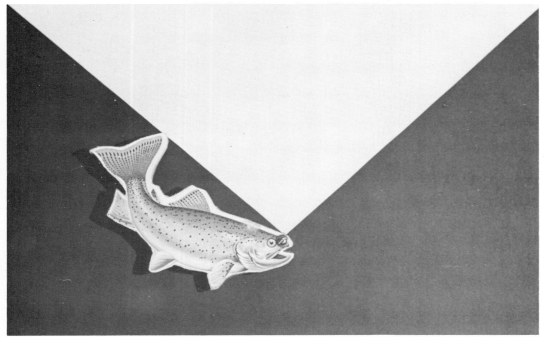

Felix can, however, enlarge the window by going deeper. The widening of the base of the cone is automatic because the angle remains constant.

Or, he can diminish the window when he rises to the surface. Changes in the size of the window are automatic as he rises or drops.

This is a slant tank. It is a watertight box with a slanting window at one end to permit examination of the water's surface through the trout's window and to observe the opaque area around the window that mirrors the bottom of the stream. It is not a new device but its great benefits have been enjoyed by only a few people since its invention. It has some drawbacks but it is the most convenient arrangement for inspecting a trout's underwater world that I know. To be sure, we cannot penetrate his mind and discover his thinking but we can certainly examine the geometry of his watery existence and appraise the physical laws and rules by which he is bound and forced to see whether he likes it or not. This is a far better device than plate glass or salad bowls. No system of fly-tying should ever be advanced without some pertinent relation to the effects of refraction. We shall see in the following illustrations not only how and where a trout sees the fly but also how a fly should be designed to meet with his views.

I have filled the tank with water. In the bottom of the tank I have placed a piece of paper with the word *mirror* written on it. When we look up through the slanting window, we shall see the letters reversed and reflected back from the opaque mirror that surrounds the trout's window. A trout can see outside the water only by those incident or direct rays that penetrate the water. These are limited to a small area at any given point and form a circular area above his position. He encounters this window wherever he goes. There is a mirror surrounding the window because the direct rays at any spot strike the bottom of the stream and are reflected back to the surface but they are so weakened that they cannot get through. There is no place for them to go but backward, therefore reflecting to the trout everything on the bottom of the stream. That is how he gets a rather murky-looking mirror all around his window.

On the surface of the water I have placed a dry fly, tied thorax style, so that it rides on hackle alone with tails and body free of the water just as a natural mayfly does.

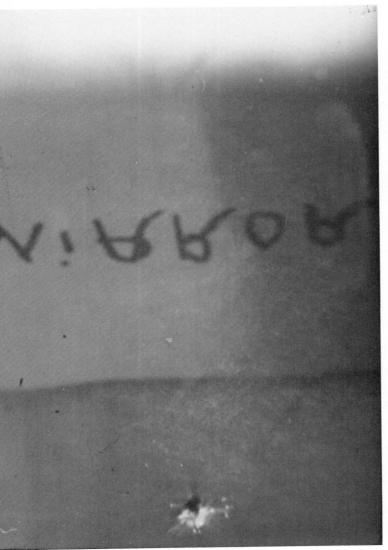 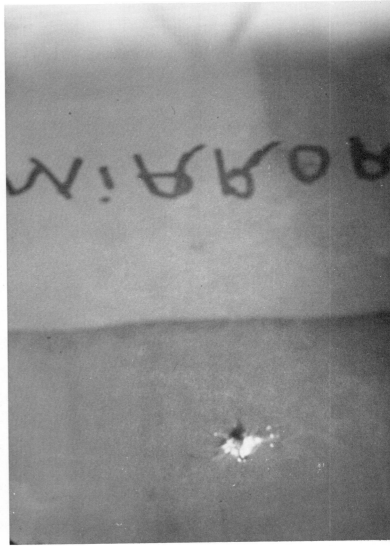

Now we are looking up through the water to the surface and we see the word *mirror* reflected back from the mirror itself. At the top of the picture a clear segment of the window is shown. At the bottom there is a shapeless blob, containing a small bright spot. That is the fly that I placed on the surface of the water and it is completely invisible to the trout except as a shapeless blob.

The bright spot is a meniscus-type lens formed by the pressing feet or hackle of the fly. It makes a condenser that pulsates and signals the approach of the fly to the trout. It is correctly described as a light pattern.

As the fly on the surface moves on the current toward the window, the wings begin to appear in the window as though detached from the body. The trout is actually beginning to see around that corner that I mentioned and is looking at the top of the fly, not the bottom, as is popularly believed.

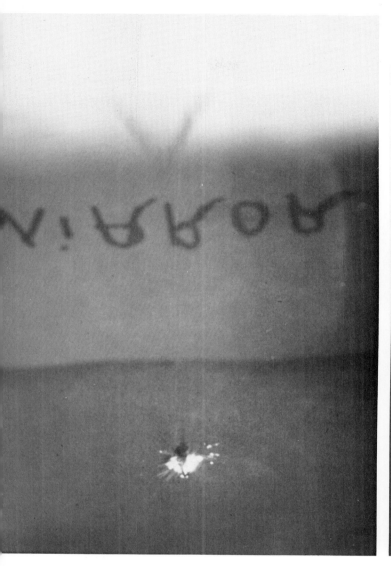

As the fly moves toward the window the wings enlarge above a rather fuzzy, smoky-looking band around the edge of the window. There has been much speculation about this fuzzy edge. It appears in all photographs of flies made by everyone who has experimented with the slant tank. Many theories have been advanced to explain this fuzz, but I am convinced that it is nothing but a photographic effect.

In my experiments, when the camera lens was focused on the horizon through the tank, the fuzziness disappeared. When the camera lens was refocused back to the edge of the window and the fly, the fuzziness reappeared with an irregular outline corresponding to the peaks and valleys of the horizon. This simply means that the lens, positioned only a few inches away from the window's edge, does not have enough depth of field to keep the horizon and the window's edge in sharp focus at the same time. In the photographs, where the lens is focused sharply on the fly and the edge of the window, the reappearance of the fuzzy band is nothing but the presence of the horizon thrown completely out of focus; it is therefore unidentifiable. Any good photographer understands this and often uses this technique to throw a background out of focus in order to emphasize the foreground.

The fly continues to move toward the edge of the window and, of course, the wings continue to grow in size. The wings will also become a little more distinct as they move closer to the window because there is less and less refractive effect as the fly advances toward the center of the window where there is no refraction at all. The bottom of the tank is still being reflected and in addition there is a black bar that is a caulked joint in the bottom. The black lines in the window are nearby telephone lines coming into view.

Finally, the light pattern and wings come together and for the first time the complete fly is visible to the trout. The fly is now at the edge of the window close to the fuzzy rim. This visible fuzziness does not actually affect the fish's view of the fly. But there is an invisible fuzzy band that does affect the view of the dun fly. It derives from the fact that the more oblique the rays of light are, that is, entering the water at a low angle, close to the surface, the more the refraction increases and the image carried by these rays becomes more indistinct. Alfred Ronalds told us this some one hundred and forty years ago. That is why a trout cannot get a clear view of the fly and the photographer cannot get a sharp picture no matter how good the equipment or how carefully he focuses on the fly, as E. R. Hewitt also discovered. As the fly moves toward the center of the window, the light rays are less oblique, there is less refraction, and the fly becomes very sharp and distinct, but the trout *does not inspect* the fly in the center of the window as we shall see. Now take a good hard look at this photograph. The fly certainly looks as though you are viewing it "head to head" at eye level on the water's surface and yet this photograph was shot from the underside of the tank with the lens pointing upward at the steep angle of 48½ degrees.

You are, indeed, looking at the fly "head to head," but that is because refraction has caused it to appear tilted, head down, as though sliding downhill. You are looking and seeing the top and sides of the body as well as all the wings.

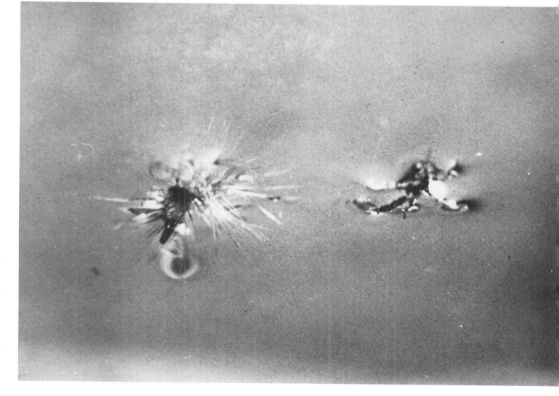

This is a very interesting photograph because it shows very little difference between the natural and artificial as they float on the surface outside the window. On the left is an artificial, on the right a natural Hendrickson dun. Neither is visible to the trout other than as a little shapeless blob.

The Double Image

There remains one vexing and nagging question to be resolved; one that serious students and observers have been debating and pondering for decades. It concerns the double image of the wet fly or nymph that occurs when the sunk fly is close to the underside of the surface and being reflected in the mirror. How does the trout know which one to take?

All of us have seen that double image, and over many years many curious and improbable explanations of it have been given. As I have often stated, the chief fault of all observers is the failure to study the window in motion. The answer to that age-old question is simple and very plain. The window is a clear area with no mirror effects; it stays with the trout wherever he goes and stays in the same upright attitude above him no matter how he twists and turns. There is enough width in the window above him to overlap objects in front of him, behind him, and to the side of him. As he moves toward any object near the surface, the advancing window dissolves the mirror so that when the trout reaches the fly the overlap portion of the window replaces the mirror and reveals only one image, the real image that the trout takes. It is as simple as that. You can simulate very well all the conditions of the trout's window by placing a flashlight above your head with the beam aimed at the ceiling in a fixed attitude. Then move about—up, down, or any direction laterally. You will see all the changes that I have described.

It is an inescapable conclusion that the trout places the fly always at the edge of the window for all purposes: viewing, inspecting, and taking. He does not use the clear central area of the window. If he did, he would be handicapping himself severely. Older and earlier observers treated the phenomenon of the window as though it were some form of still life, like a painting. It must be considered in terms of movement, constant movement. It would be virtually impossible for a trout to take a fly if he placed it above his head in the center of his window. At the shallow depth where he inspects, about three inches, the fly in the center of the window would probably be invisible, because of the blind spot above his head. More importantly, because we are dealing with movement, the trout must remain below or downstream from the insect in order to intercept (that word again) the moving fly. Like the wing shot who must hit a moving bird with a moving gun in order to get ahead of the bird, the trout must get or keep ahead of a moving fly with his moving body else the fly escapes him. Keeping the fly at the upstream side of the window solves this problem for him. The downstream, or reverse, strike is very much like the gunners' straightaway shot. It needs no fine calculations in swing or timing. It is simply an extended point-blank strike.

This is Felix again. He is advancing toward the double image of a wet fly. The lower one is the real fly. The upper one is the reversed mirror image of the real fly. Which one does he take?

There is no problem. The advancing window has reached and overlapped the fly, dissolving the mirror and the mirrored image, leaving only the single image of the real fly that Felix takes without hesitation.

WHERE DOES THE TROUT SEE THE FLY?

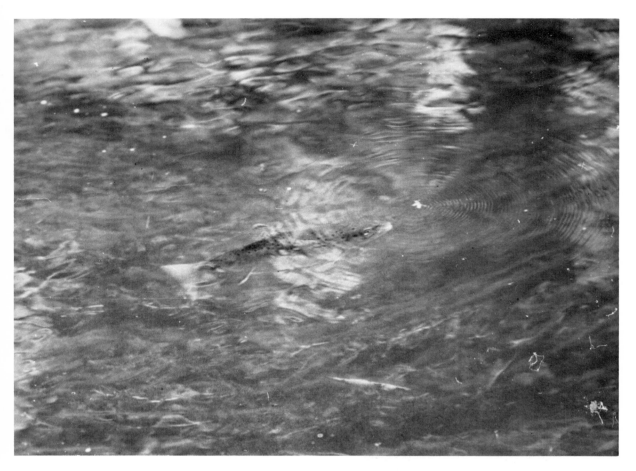

This is the most meaningful photograph of a trout that the reader will ever see. Once, while photographing, I saw the fly in the picture fall into the water upriver, long before the trout did. As I watched I could see the trout begin his rise when the fly came within the range of his vision. When he had risen to the position pictured, he stopped short and began to drift downstream, backward, tail first with the fly, while maintaining precisely the distance and attitude shown in the picture. I watched carefully as he drifted backward, and when he was directly opposite and at right angles to the film plane, I snapped the shutter and got this picture. The trout drifted a great distance in this way, perhaps twenty feet, obviously inspecting the fly very carefully. I had seen this many times before and I have other pictures similar to this.

This is the classical attitude of inspection, repeated over and over again and especially important here because it was a locked-in attitude and distance from the fly. I stared at the picture many times, studying it and making rough diagrams with pencil and protractor until finally some really significant facts began to emerge.

Encouraged by these preliminaries, I went to a professional draftsman and asked him to draw a vertical angle of 97.12° to represent the trout's window. There is some small difference of opinion about the correct angle of the window, varying from 97° to 97.12°. I do not believe that the fractional difference matters.

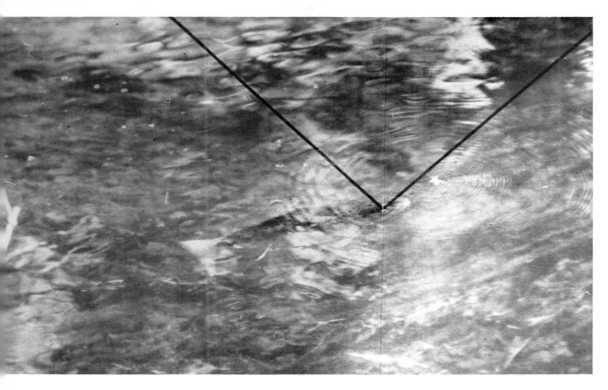

After receiving the drawing of the vertical angle I pinned it to a wall, locating the pin where the two construction lines, the vertical and the horizontal, intersected at the top of the picture or base of the angle. Then I hung a plumb bob from the pin and swung the drawing from side to side until the vertical construction line, bisecting the angle, coincided exactly with the plumb line.

Next I projected a picture of the drifting trout and fly on the simulated window, approximating the size of the trout as closely as possible and adjusting the position of his eye to coincide with the apex of the vertical angle. After this procedure, I stood back to view the result and was not really surprised to see, what may be startling to the reader, that the fly appears to be outside his window. Let us leave it there for the time being and go to the next development.

With further reference to the draftsman's construction lines, I drew a horizontal line W W' to represent the surface of the water on which the fly is riding. Next I drew a line L L' at 10° to the surface to represent the light rays that enter and penetrate the surface at the lowest angle. It is very obvious, I think, that these lowest rays have met and carried the image of the fly downward to the eye of the trout. The redirection of the image takes place at W because of the effect of refraction. The trout is seeing around a corner!

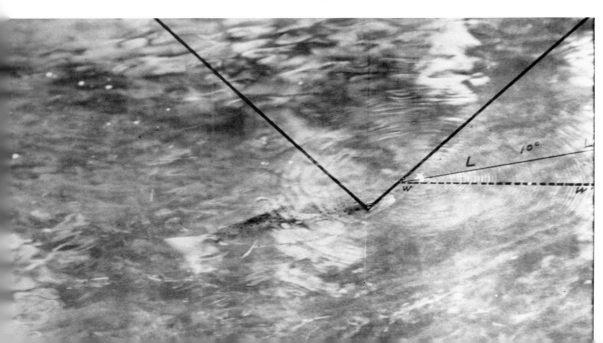

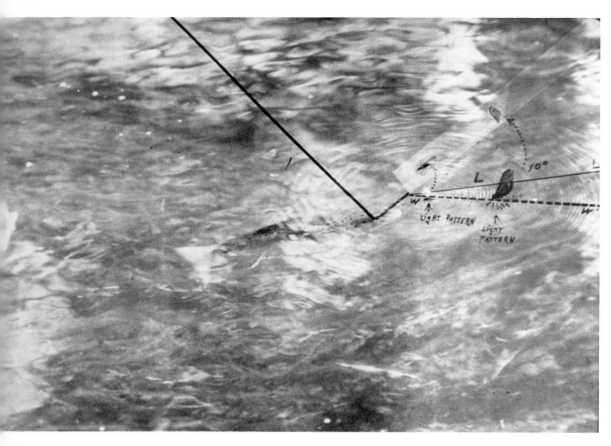

In this picture I went a little further and added something new—a real mayfly pasted on the water's surface. As the reader can see, the lowest light ray encounters the larger fly a greater distance from the window, but only the upper portion of the wing's image is carried to the trout's eye exactly as we saw it through the slant tank. As the fly moves toward the window, more and more of the top of the fly is transmitted to the trout's eye until the entire fly is finally revealed at the edge of the window as we saw in the slant tank photograph.

One other effect is shown in this picture. A trout thinks he sees in straight lines just as man thinks. Neither he nor we are aware that we can see around corners. The last turn that the ray of light took before it met his eye determines the apparent position of the fly's image. Thus, if the line from his eye to W is extended infinitely, the fly on the surface of the water appears to be high in the air above him, and when he takes the fly he is behaving very much like a small boy catching peanuts out of the air with his mouth. And note how the projected image gives him a *topside view*!

There may be some error in the position of the fly because of the effect of refraction on the trout itself. To determine what error there was, if any, I conducted the following experiment.

A tub was filled with water. A trout's "eye" was anchored in the bottom. A vertical angle of 97.12° was constructed and anchored with the eye at the apex. A ruler was floated adjacent to the arms of the angle. The picture shown here, after consulting the spirit levels and angle marks on the panhead of my tripod, was shot to simulate exactly the elevation (45°) of the camera, the correct angle of the fish to the film plane, and size of the fish.

As the reader can see from the experiment, the effect of refraction is to push the eye up toward the surface. The apparently bent arms of the white angle reveal this. Accordingly, a false impression is created indicating a higher position in the water than the real position. Since all conditions in the experiment were controlled to simulate the conditions in the fish picture, I made some careful measurements. The apparent depth of the eye measured from the ruler's edge was 1 5/16 inch when the experiment was projected on a screen, life size. Measured in the tub, the actual depth of the eye was 3 inches.

I got almost exactly the same result with the fish picture when it was projected life size on a screen. The apparent depth of the eye was 1 3/8 inch. Therefore, the real depth of the trout in the picture would be about the same as the eye in the tub. Accordingly, I dropped the vertical angle to the 3-inch depth indicated and found that the fly came to the inside edge of the window, probably sitting on the fuzzy edge of the rim, as we saw it in the last photograph of the slant tank.

The diagram shows the shift.

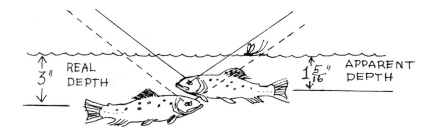

In view of all that has been said and shown in this chapter, there are a number of strong inferences that cannot be ignored or lightly dismissed.

1. The dun, riding lightly above the surface film, is never clearly defined at the point where the trout sees, inspects, and takes the insect. Form and behavior are the most important elements. Any meticulous attention to color or detail is wasted effort. The artificial dun pattern must be kept above the surface film. If the dun breaks through the film, *you are showing the trout too much!*

2. Anything that breaks through the surface film is no longer obscured by the oblique rays or the diffusion above the film. Accordingly, spinners, large terrestrials, emergers, and rising nymphs are extremely well defined as to color, form, and parts. Special attention should be given to the remarkable transformation of the spinner wings as seen below the surface film —and explained in Chapter 5.

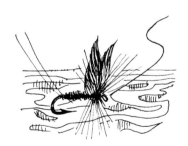

Chapter Three

Fishing to the Ring of the Rise

I HAVE WATCHED A GREAT MANY THOUSANDS OF TROUT RISES AND AS I watched with a growing awareness I became more and more impressed with the complicated nature of a trout's rise pattern, even the simple rise which is not really simple. Stop to consider the problems confronting a trout when he wants to take a tiny bite of food—the fly is moving, the water is moving, his entire body is moving, and he must determine precisely a point of interception. What's more, the interception is accomplished not by some large natural or artificial device such as a landing net

or baseball glove but with a comparatively small mouth, allowing him only a few square inches to trap an insect. Consider, too, that the interception is often accomplished in flowing water of great turbulence, causing the fly to bob and swoop wildly as it passes. It is no wonder that trout sometimes miss the fly in these circumstances.

I have likened the trout's existence to that of the crack wing shot and the trained baseball player, both of whom must acquire the same remarkable skill. Even more appropriate, trout require the same kind of proficiency displayed by birds of prey. I have always been fascinated by the performance of nighthawks, at dusk and in the early morning hours, diving with terrific speed from a great height in the sky, sounding like the bull-roarer toy of my boyhood, to intercept the fluttery, erratic flight of an insect with unbelievable accuracy.

On analysis the procedure of each of these performers is exactly the same. The first movement of the interceptor is to get up speed and direction toward the moving object in a general way. As the interceptor moves toward the object, small adjustments in speed and direction are being constantly made. Eye and brain and muscle combine to make lightning-fast changes. None of these changes in speed or direction are well defined. There is no sharp line of demarcation between them. They blend into one another, and altogether they present the aspect of one smooth continuous movement.

These adjustments become shorter and more precise as the distance narrows between them. Finally, all adjustments and calculations cease when the interceptor reaches point-blank range. It is hard to say what that point blank may be—a foot or two perhaps or maybe only a couple of inches. A baby trout learns this range very early in life. It is the only way he can eat—taking only the bits of food that appear immediately in front of him. With advancing age he becomes more skillful and extends this range, resulting eventually in the complicated rise pattern of the older trout.

It is at this point-blank range, this brief fragment of space-time, never forgotten, that a trout commits himself to the final thrust that may or may not result in an interception.

In most cases the trained performer—trout, man, or bird—does not miss. Indeed, when we watch with admiration the fine precision of the crack gunner or baseball player, we do not wonder that he connects so often, but all of us wonder wide-eyed and head-shaking when he misses. A miss may not be his fault. At the exact moment that he arrives at point-blank range, some vagary—a little puff of wind, for example—may divert the flying object just enough to cause a miss. In the case of the trout, here is one of the more astonishing revelations connected with the behavior of trout since the beginning of fly-fishing; it concerns the element of drag.

Drag is the dreaded black beast of the fly-fisherman's existence. We are constantly hearing about it, reading about it, and seeing it every day that we fish with flies. It exists for the wet-fly and nymph fisherman as well as the dry-fly man. Each, and every one of us, if we are serious fishermen, is always fighting it and trying to avoid it. Over a long history of fly-fishing, numerous casts have been invented, designed to circumvent this dreadful scourge.

The word *drag* is really a misnomer and does not describe all the strange things that can happen to a fly when it is connected to a leader. A fly thrown to the surface of the water by a fisherman, without any manipulation by the fisherman, can actually travel upstream or across a current. It can move downstream faster than the current or it can hang motionless in a strong current—all this as the result of the leader traveling at a different rate or direction from that of the fly. Many books by competent writers and fishermen contain learned discussions about drag and its effects. All describe the repeated refusals of a trout to accept a dragging fly, and all conclude that a dragging fly frightens the trout. I do not agree with that at all. It is true that a bungler can and often does make a slap-hard cast on top of

the trout's head that scares him out of his wits and sends him scurrying. That is not a cast. That is a menace.

I have seen many competent casters put dragging casts many times over a feeding trout, all of which were ignored but none of which put the trout down or off his feed. Very often the drag is so imperceptible that the drag is unnoticeable to the fisherman. The good caster suffers a great deal from this because his casts will have less noticeable drag than that of the novice. All of us are victims of the hidden drag. If you really want to find out the truth about this, you can try the following revealing experiment: Take a small chip of paper or wood as big as a fingernail, and toss it out into the current. Get below or downstream and make your best cast with the fly as close to the chip as possible. Watch them closely as they move along. If the fly veers away only slightly, merely an inch or two, you have a fatal drag. Don't try it only on a nice smooth straightforward current; try it in different areas. You will be astounded and perhaps depressed by the result.

If you think that I have exaggerated the problem, then I will ask you to go back and reconsider the mental and physical process which a trout always employs to take a fly; when he arrives at the point-blank range, after numerous calculations and adjustments, he is in the same position as the bird, the gunner, the baseball player. Your little bit of drag is the equivalent of the little puff of wind that caused a miss. You have not frightened the trout, you have disappointed him! What you have done is to destroy his nice calculations and to take the fly away from his predetermined point of interception. He may make one try for the fly and likely miss; thereafter he will ignore it.

You must realize that a trout cannot afford to miss very often. Because he must move his whole body to take a tiny insect, many times no bigger than the head of a pin, he is using a great deal of energy on every pass. He must have an adequate return with each effort, else he dies.

Speculations on the effect of the leader and the consequent

drag have been expressed from time to time by good writers and fishermen in fishing literature. Some of these have been somewhat overdrawn, like Major Hills's story in *A Summer on the Test*. The Major, in alleging the gut-cunning of Test trout, tells how he put the fly well to one side of a trout, showing him no gut. The fish turned out to take the fly but before doing so he (the Major says) swam around to see if there was gut on the other side. The major ends his tale by waxing indignant because he could never get anyone to believe that simple and truthful story. Though the late Major Hills was a fine writer and a real spellbinder, I wonder often if he was telling that tale with tongue in cheek.

But I am greatly impressed by frequent references to experiments made by competent fishermen-writers in which artificials, regardless of pattern, were dropped on the water, unattached to leaders, to waiting trout which took them one after another without hesitation. Those same patterns attached to leaders were refused repeatedly by the same trout.

In picture and narrative I have tried to be emphatic about the necessity for a long free float in order to overcome drag during the frequently long drift of the trout in the process of inspection, selection, and interception. In the course of many conversations and friendly disputes with other fishermen, especially Catskill fishermen, I am often confronted with the argument that what I say about limestone trout may be true but that Catskill trout are different and do not behave in the same way. They are wrong. Trout are the same the world over, no matter where you put them. In this connection, there is no better authority than George La Branche, principal architect of the early American style of fishing the rough mountain waters of New York and northeastern Pennsylvania. Those who have read his fine book (*The Dry Fly and Fast Water*) have either forgotten or ignored what he had to say about the habits of feeding trout in those waters. Go back and read Chapter 2 of his book in which he relates his astonishment at discovering his mountain

trout (brown trout) drifting with the insect as much as eight or ten feet, turning to take the insect in reverse or headed downstream just as I have described the limestone trout.

George La Branche had very good eyesight but no better than many other fishermen. He also had that wonderful faculty of being able to interpret shadowy, obscure movements under the water's surface that told him where to place his fly. And he also had a remarkable skill in placing his fly in the proper groove of the current with free float. I personally witnessed that skill. Remember, too, that this was a great fisherman who used only a few patterns of fly. His entire fishing life was a severe contrast with the modern, narrow, oversimplistic approach of relying on pattern alone, in which all too frequently the fishing scene reveals the fisherman frantically changing flies instead of observing the trout and exploring all the available options in the all-important matter of presentation.

The word *presentation* is bandied about a great many times in fishing literature. I am not sure that anyone, including myself, knows all that the word implies. In many cases the word is used without supplying the specifics, as though mere mention of the word is enough to explain all. Early fishing literature, for at least 400 years, had little or nothing to say about it. There existed nothing more than long lists of recipes for fly patterns until the time of Halford in England and La Branche in America. From that time onward a few writers have become increasingly aware that something more, much more than fly pattern is needed.

Certainly the proper kind of a cast is an important element. Here I shall interpose a quotation from Major Hills's *A Summer on the Test*, a completely believable quotation this time and one that is typical of his vigorous, sometimes explosive and electric style.

"There remain always before you the three great mountain peaks of casting, which most of us spend all our lives trying to climb, sometimes advancing, sometimes alas, slipping back. The first of these peaks is the capacity to put your fly always straight into a strong wind, straight into it and not across it: and a real heavy wind: not a fresh breeze, or any nonsense of that sort, but what our Caroline ancestors called a whistling wind; the second, the ability to throw a very slack line and yet drop your fly time after time on the same spot; and the third, the skill to cock your fly, at any rate more often than not. These are stern and lofty peaks and none but the gifted can surmount them. But though only a few can reach the top, at any rate all can climb the foothills: and when you have done this, you will catch fish. . . ." Major Hills said this some fifty-odd years ago and said it well. I subscribe to all of it and would emphasize especially the requirements of *extreme accuracy* and the ability to throw a *very slack line.*

In this chapter I shall try to show how some of this may be achieved.

The most difficult waters I have ever fished are the clear, weedy, slow-moving limestone waters. Coming as I did, from rapid freestone waters, I was ill-prepared for the shocking behavior of my straightforward casts on the treacherously calm surface of these meadow limestones. I do not suggest that any kind of a sloppy cast will do on the rough freestoners, or that artfulness is not needed, merely that the limestoners are much more difficult by comparison.

In due time the reasons for my failures became apparent and I had to set about to overcome them.

The surface currents in these waters are entirely different from anything that I had ever experienced. They are created in different ways. Submerged weed beds with multiple narrow channels meandering back and forth between the beds create many subsurface currents. Some kinds of weeds grow above the water and create multiple surface currents. The subsurface currents are often diverted upward to join and mingle with multiple surface currents.

There is no permanence in these effects. The weed beds grow

rapidly, changing the lies from week to week, obliterating old lies and creating new ones elsewhere.

The few straightforward currents are often driven into a large obstruction such as a weed bed or logjam, causing the current to veer sharply and drive straight across streams to the other bank. Add to all this numerous backwaters or eddies where the trout face down rather than upstream and you have some idea of the difficulties involved. Moreover, these trout are well fed, have ample time to inspect and accept or reject the fly.

The habit of drifting with the insect, natural or artificial, is very pronounced in these waters. All this adds up to some kind of a nightmare, especially for the casual stranger who often stands there with a helpless look and sometimes turns and leaves. Obviously, what is wanted here is a dragless, free float to drift uninhibited for a long time. Or to hang in the backwaters to drift about aimlessly for just as long.

I was not so uninformed in those early days as not to know that there were many special casts designed to overcome drag and float problems. I knew about curve casts and kick-back casts and later even about the kind of a cast where the rod is wiggled from side to side while the cast is in midair supposedly to put waves in the line, thus allowing the fly to float longer while the waves pay out into the current.

But how much good is a curve cast if half of it hangs up on a big patch of watercress against which a trout is feeding? What good is a wiggle cast if 90 percent of the width of the river is a vast weed bed upon which all the wiggles fall. No! What is needed is something that allows a more compact concentration of loose coils very close to the fly. The only cast that I finally settled upon is variously described as a bounce or kick-back cast. It has served me well for many years and many trout have fallen to that cast. It is not a difficult cast to make. The final or power cast is driven rod high parallel with the water. The rod point is stopped high, thus killing the headway of the cast, causing the front and or leader portion to kick backward, thus

allowing the leader and some of the line to fall in compact loose coils on the water. It worked very well for most circumstances, giving me the longer floats that I wanted so badly.

In order to make this case even more effective I resorted to heavier and heavier lines, and stiffer rods. Eventually I was using a powerful weapon, throwing a line with a belly diameter of .070. In view of present practices this may sound excessive especially with terminal tackle of 6 or 7X and size 20 or even smaller flies. Actually it wasn't excessive. This goes back many years, in the days of pure silk lines with extremely long tapers maybe as much as thirty feet or more. It was necessary to make a cast of forty to forty-five feet in order to get the belly out of the guides, thus gaining enough weight to get a proper kick-back. Lightweight lines were worthless for this cast. Today with modern lines in the weight-forward class with very short front tapers this cast is efficiently done with lines of .045 or .050 diameter and rods can be correspondingly much lighter. The kick-back, or bounce-back, cast, as good as it was, was never the final answer, but I lacked a better solution until the day that the "puddle cast" was born.

Imagine the following circumstances: On the far bank there

was a solid wall of trees close to the water's edge. One tree, a willow, hung out over the water so that a wall of branches drooped downward to cover and define a considerable area of water. In that area under the willow a fine trout was rising repeatedly. It was impossible to get a cast under those branches. I lost a few flies trying to do that. Then I tried a bounce-back cast on the upstream side but it was hopeless. I needed something like a twenty-five-foot float to get to the trout. My cast would not even float halfway until it began to die and pull away from the line of drift.

Then I tried to get a bigger bounce and more slack by driving the line high in the air above the wall of trees. It did not bounce properly but fell in a dreadful looking heap on the water. I stood there looking at that mess with disgust and began to think that it was time to quit and go home. Then to my great surprise the fly detached itself from that cluster of coils and began drifting under the tree; the coils, meanwhile, were loosening and paying out into the current, allowing a tremendously long float the like of which I had never seen. The fly was not accurately placed. It was wide of the trout's line of drift but it did reach him and go past him. That was good enough for me.

I retrieved my line, went upstream, away from the trout and began to practice that same cast. I had learned on that original discovery that a hard bounce was the wrong thing to use on that high pitch. Accordingly, I experimented with a high, soft pitch and it worked like a charm. I went back to the trout, made a couple of experimental casts on the upstream side of the leaning tree until I had the range and the feel of the thing, quickly recovering the fly each time, not permitting it to float until I felt that it was just right. Finally, I made a high, soft pitch and let everything fall in a heap that looked good to me. I let the fly follow its way under the tree, through that tunnel of branches. I watched transfixed, as the fly made that long, long journey with all my hopes riding with it. Imagine my delight when I heard a soft, slurping sound, lifted the rod, and found that I was fast to a good trout.

I shall now try to analyze and explain the execution of the puddle cast as best I can. Incidentally, this cast works just as well for the wet-fly fisherman as well as it does for the dry-fly man. The wet-fly man must, of course, use a fast-sinking wet fly or nymph.

In the usual technique of dry-fly fishing, the caster makes numerous false casts in a rather easy manner for the purpose of drying the fly and getting the range. These false casts are ordinarily made in a horizontal direction parallel with the surface of the water. The final cast to the trout is a much-speeded-up punch shot designed to straighten the leader and get the fly on target. The puddle cast is a soft cast very much like a false cast. The punch shot is eliminated. Furthermore, the final false cast is delivered much higher than horizontal, perhaps 20 or 25 degrees higher. The leader should never straighten out. The fly should not travel any further than the end of the line. At the end of the pitch the heavier line begins to fall first while the fly hangs suspended momentarily in the air. When the line is approximately halfway down to the water the entire leader looks like it is suspended in midair, perpendicular to the water. Then the entire leader collapses softly into a compact cluster of loose coils. It looks terrible but it really works. I have never had the fly or the leader locked in the tangle. The action of the water will always separate them and move them along.

When the high pitch is made the rod point must be stopped very early and must not be allowed to come forward as for the standard kind of horizontal cast else the high angle cannot be achieved.

The puddle cast has one serious deficiency. It is very difficult to manage in a strong wind. For wind casts and a very slack line there is no better cast than the kick-back cast, driven hard with a narrow forward loop—but you will never get the immense amount of slack and long, drag-free float that you get with the wonderful puddle cast.

Chapter Four

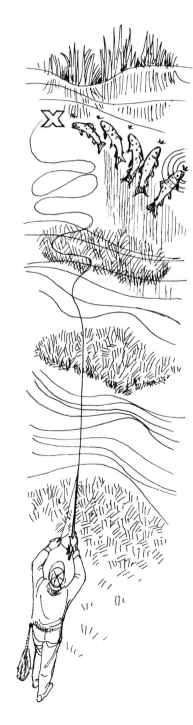

Rod Function: Rod Design

IN 1889 R. C. LEONARD, A TOURNAMENT CASTER, STEPPED TO THE platform without a reel on his rod and simply coiled the line at his feet. With that abbreviated rig he proceeded to smash all existing distance records, including his own, by a wide margin. It was a shocking thing to competitors and spectators alike. It was a momentous discovery from which not only tournament casters but fishermen as well should have profited. That early-day pioneer discovered an extremely important principle in rod dynamics. It amounts to this: That the caster must move the useless weight below the hand as well as the useful weight above the hand; that the removal of dead weight below the hand helped to overcome inertia more quickly, increasing the tip speed, thus imparting a greater velocity to the projectile or fly line. It should have been a valuable lesson to everyone, but it wasn't. It remained only among the tournament casters for many years.

If you examine the books and catalogs of those early days you will discover that manufacturers and fishermen-writers discussed very learnedly and extensively such things as "fulcrum point," "counterpoise," "balancing the fly rod," and "letting the rod do the work," none of which has any merit whatsoever. Not until very recently has there been an awareness of this valid principle. It is evidenced by the availability of numerous fine, very lightweight reels on the market today. In view of this trend I should not be discussing this subject at all, except for the fact that I am frequently surprised by the comments of writers and the recommendations of suppliers or manufacturers prescribing a specific size and weight of reel to balance a particular rod. There can be no such thing as balance in a fly rod. There can never be a fixed "fulcrum point." Every inch that the cast is lengthened or shortened changes the alleged balance and every unnecessary ounce in an unnecessarily heavy reel dampens and degrades the cast. If you wish to explore this a little further, you can try an experiment as I did some years ago. If you have or can borrow enough reels, let us say in two-ounce increments, all the way from the lightest, about two ounces, to something about eight or nine ounces, you will have enough to make the experiment. Use the same weight of line on the same fly rod for all trials. With the lightest reels the casts are sharply and cleanly delivered flat out with enough velocity to turn over the leaders. You also get a tighter front bow if you want it. As the reels get heavier there is a noticeable lagging in the forward loop until finally with the heaviest reel there is decided dropping of the loop, and probably a failure to turn over the leader properly. This effect is most pronounced on long casts. And

consider how much worse it could be with those reels that were manufactured with a hollow arbor into which the purchaser was urged to pour lead pellets through a little trapdoor in order to correct the balance of his fly rod!

You can suit yourself about these matters but for me there is only one sound system and that is: Use the lightest possible reel of good quality and adequate capacity no matter how long or heavy the rod may be. There is no problem about getting quality and as for capacity, you have immense control over that, too! Accordingly, one of my very best combinations is a tiny two-ounce reel on a nine-foot rod. Adequate capacity is obtained by using a weight-forward line. Make a cast long enough to be handled comfortably by you and your favorite trout rig. Cut off all the running line remaining on the reel and fill the reel with fine Dacron backing line, a superb material, far better than anything obtainable in the old days. You will have enough capacity to handle the biggest trout that swims and additionally a backing that can function as a shooting line if you really need a few extra feet.

I am a firm believer in weight-forward lines, particularly the kind designated as rocket tapers. I do not know why anyone would want to use double tapers and deny himself the blessings of the weight-forward line. The alleged advantages of the double taper are illusory. They represent extra weight and bulk. They require larger, hence, heavier reels to contain that bulk. There is little merit in the claim that modifications of the cast with movements of an accessory or adjectival nature are accomplished better with double tapers than with weight-forward lines—if such things are really necessary.

The very substantial advantage of being able to use a very light reel, for reasons given above, far outweigh any other considerations.

In my own practice, not only have I limited the number of reels that I need but lines as well. Accordingly, I have designed all my trout rods to carry only one weight of line, a 5 weight. A

6 weight system would probably work just as well on the theory that these two weights are the most efficient of all sizes: they will return greater dividends to the caster in terms of delicacy of delivery, wind-bucking qualities, length of cast, and the use of lighter rods. All my trout rods from six to nine feet handle only one reel and line size. It has been an entirely satisfactory system.

I have mentioned that old saw about "letting the rod do the work." That idea still prevails. The rod cannot make a cast any more than a baseball bat can hit a home run by itself. It is the caster's own muscle and energy that makes the cast. The rod, because of its small mass in cross section, cannot store up and release enough energy to make any kind of a cast. Robert Crompton once conducted a public experiment in which an ultrastiff rod was anchored upright in a vise, then the line was drawn backward to create maximum bend in the rod. On being released the line was dragged forward a short distance but could not get past the rod.

These are interesting and significant aspects in rod function and all fly-rod fishermen should be concerned with them.

My own interest eventually went further than these subsidiary matters for I was finally, some forty-five years ago, induced to become an amateur rod-builder. Actually, it was something that I undertook under a kind of duress.

I had become enamored of the dry fly very early in life, but it was a time when very little was known about it. It was only a few short years before my own involvement that the books of Gill, La Branche, and Rhead had been published. They were helpful but I did not realize how very much they were limited until later years, when in the light of my own experience I was able to overcome many difficulties, mostly on my own initiative.

Perhaps the most severe limitation placed on all of us at that time was in the matter of tackle, in just about every department, particularly, proper dry-fly rods. The rods available in those

Lo! the poor fisherman, contemplating the numerous hazards that confront him: the wall of trees and weeds behind him to catch his backcast; the profusion of weed beds waiting to trap his forward cast; the many refuges into which a hooked and frantic trout can dive and smash the leader.

Hip deep in meadow weeds that can trap a long backcast and the challenge of striking a rising trout against the far bank seventy feet away, as the fisherman has done here, makes the long tip-action rod the ideal choice for this kind of work.

days were long—nine feet or more, heavy, very slow to respond, and extremely tiresome under the burden of the numerous false casts that a dry-fly fisherman must make in a long fishing day. It was a lucky thing for me that I did not have access to the English dry-fly books in that period else I might have started my career with some frightful instrument anywhere from eleven to fifteen feet long. So, my impatience with existing and available rods induced me to try my hand at rod-building.

I started with solid wood—greenheart hickory, lemonwood. These were comparatively easy to work; planing, rounding, and tapering presented no great problem since I had some skill and experience as an amateur woodworker. Eventually, I had to abandon these woods because they were unsatisfactory on many counts. The experience was valuable. I learned a great deal about rod action. Without training as an engineer, the knowledge acquired is gained through the empirical process. It is a matter of trial and error: sensing and feeling the changes needed, requiring, of course, the ability to execute those changes in order to improve each new model.

I learned two important things in those days: The length of rod had to be held within proper bounds and a suitable material must be used. There is a third most important lesson that I shall discuss later in this chapter. It was apparent to me that the only suitable material was bamboo. Accordingly, I made the giant leap into the making of split-bamboo fly rods.

Here again, the long rod held in a low arc allows the angler to guide his fish gently and skillfully around the many treacherous weed beds and other obstructions in the stream. Only the mild resistance of the reel is used here.

Still holding his fish under the low arc of the long rod, the angler has finally reached some open water where the fish can be landed safely. This is the way to prevent the vicious tail-slapping against the leader often used by big trout.

I will not bore the reader with all my trials and tribulations in that endeavor; I will say only briefly that such a task is a huge undertaking, full of disappointments and many frustrations. And if you are a perfectionist, it might be many years before you achieve a satisfactory product. Getting the right tools is a big hurdle in itself, including a split steel planing mold and a gluing machine, which I had to make for myself as a teen-age boy. With those trying days in mind, I shudder inside a little when I am approached by individuals expressing a desire to make split-bamboo fly rods.

Now let us consider one of the three important considerations in the manufacture of fly rods—the material. It is common knowledge that manufacturers of fly rods are still deeply concerned with the problem of finding suitable rod material. We have been through a long history of searching, involving exotic and native woods, whalebone, bamboo, steel, glass, and now graphite. Bamboo is still the great standard against which all other materials are measured. At its best it makes a magnificent weapon. It lost ground for a time because being a natural product, it lacks uniformity, is incapable of being mass-produced for quality, is subject to many deteriorating influences, and is costly to manufacture—but then no one would say that Stradivarius violins can be mass-produced either. Rods made of synthesized materials were and are a great boon to fishermen because of durability, uniformity, and cheaper manufacture. But strange to relate there are fishermen who would rather fish with a second-rate bamboo than with the best rod of any other material just as there are gunners who won't shoot with any design except the traditional and aristocratic double gun.

Bamboo, being a natural product, like flesh and blood, can establish a greater affinity with its owner than with any other material. There can be a powerful personal bond between them, an identification, that lets the caster feel that the rod is an extension of his own personality. It goes beyond mere pride of ownership.

This is the romantic side of bamboo ownership, of course, and if bamboo is to maintain its status as a material, it must stand or fall on the basis of measured mechanical efficiency against any other material. And today, with all its faults, I do not hesitate to say, emphatically, that nothing on this earth is more suited for a given job than bamboo is for fly rods. I say this because bamboo has one outstanding and desirable property not contained in other materials: It has that wonderful property of allowing the caster to deliver a cushioned stroke. This is a priceless quality, or property, that forgives all its many faults. The reason for this lies in its peculiar physical structure which is like other grasses and reedlike growths.

The outer skin is a hard siliceous coat of no value. Next to this is a cambium-like layer with a paperlike texture. Both of these are removed in rod-building. The remainder is composed of two very dissimilar components. One of these is the bundle of long hard fibers mostly concentrated near the outer skin. The other is a soft pithy material that serves as a bond and matrix in which the long fibers are embedded but separated from one another by the pithy material. The valuable dense outer layer of fibers is not much more than 1/16 inch thick. This is a very fortunate arrangement because the interior of the rod when completed becomes nothing but soft pith, keeping the rod light, and gives the hard outer layer some place to go during the violent displacement of the fibers when the rod is under tension and compression in the act of casting, besides which there are no useful dynamics in the center of the rod. It is a dead area. That is why older techniques of double-building and steel-centering were worthless and actually harmful. In the act of casting the stresses created by bending cause those long fibers to move in different directions—sideways, vertically, and horizontally— pushing hard against the pith which is so soft that it can be cut with your fingernail. That is the cushion against which the hard fibers are working. As a result of this cushion, reaction or recovery from the violent shifting and bending is delayed and dampened so much that the line or projectile is allowed to go smoothly on the way while it is still in contact with the rod tip. What's more, the line goes on its way unhampered by wavy impulses because the tip does not vibrate or react violently. That is what is meant by a cushioned stroke.

It is the closest thing I know to a denial of Newton's second law of motion. To be sure, the reaction is there but it is held back and delayed or softened even from the slight pressure of the running line. It is remarkably similar to the sudden forward motion of the barrel of a big naval gun, after which it recoils slowly and smoothly against the cushion of a spring-loaded carriage to dampen and kill the vibrations.

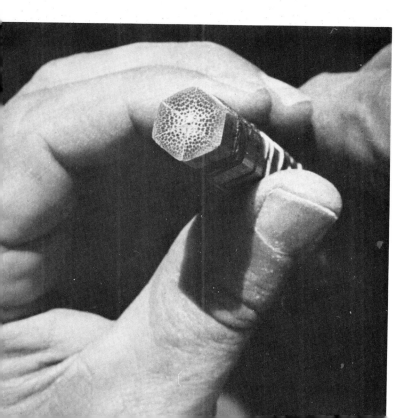

Soft pith, hard fiber, and good craftsmanship combine to create a miracle of strength and brilliant action in the modern split-bamboo fly rod.

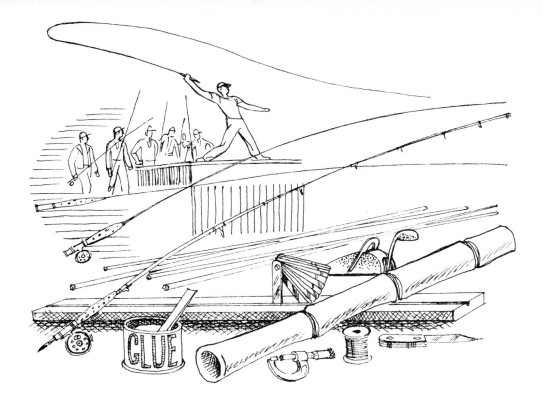

Rod manufacturers have known about this for some time and have been battling to obtain that same beautiful performance with new materials from time to time. My own belief concerning these efforts is that it is a mistake to rely on homologous or single-structured materials. Nature's plan, in bamboo, seems like a far better avenue of approach.

That pith that I have been discussing in the split-cane rod is a contradiction in name and function. It contributes to both the weakest and strongest elements in the bamboo rod. When you stop to consider you must realize that the entire structure of that fine instrument that you have used, possibly for many years, is a miracle of strength held together by nothing but a piece of punk. It begins to break down, immediately, with the first cast from a new rod and continues to deteriorate at a pace that is dependent on the amount of abuse that it gets from the owner.

There are many ways to abuse a rod beyond the limits of adhesion between pith and fiber. I have seen most of them: skull-dragging big fish such as salmon; tugging violently when the fly is hung in a tree; overburdening the rod with heavy lines; trying to retrieve a very long cast, and many others. I have seen a fine rod ruined on one fishing trip. On the other hand, a split-cane rod can last a lifetime with decent use. The limits of adhesion between pith and fiber are often reached without any visible evidence. Many a rod has a broken back without sign of rupture. In fact, bamboo rods do not rupture unless ruined in manufacture by heat treatment, undersize ferrules, or glue failure. The weak pith prevents rupture. All wood products begin to break on the concave or compression side of a bent piece. The collapse of fibers forms a hard wedge that pushes up against the convex side until the limits of tension are reached and the fibers in tension are rent asunder. The soft pith on the compression side cannot form a hard wedge to cause such a rupture. That is how the pith contributes, in a negative way, to bamboo's enormous resistance to fracture. But as I have said, many a rod has a broken back even though the exterior appears to be immaculate. Such a rod will no longer cast accurately but will follow the weak side and weave in the act of casting. The same thing applies to glass or any other material, except that there is a difference in the way that the breakdown occurs.

I have indicated that length is one of the three important considerations in rod design and rod function. Length must be regarded in two aspects: one, as a limiting factor in the use of rod materials and the energy output of the caster, and two, as a factor in the dynamics of rod function.

It is obvious, I think, that any lightweight material, highly resistant to bending, can be made longer and be kept within the bounds of the caster's ability to move it and move it fast than any material of an opposite nature. Bamboo, glass, and now graphite have this valuable attribute. Hollow thin-walled tubes, other than steel, and natural growths with punky interiors have been the best solution for obtaining length and minimizing weight. Additionally, such materials afford a minimal diameter or cross section to overcome wind resistance, an extremely important consideration in distance casting. Any *small* reduction is a tremendous advantage. In this respect fiber glass has been good. I think that bamboo is better and graphite, at this point, has the smallest diameter for length and stiffness that I have yet seen. Whether or not graphite rods, with that very thin-walled construction, can stand the harsh judgment of time and use I do not know. They are too new to be assessed; besides, I have no experience with them.

Length as a dynamic factor in rod function is little understood. Static length means little or nothing. Rods are described in the catalogs as having a specific length, for example, of six, seven, eight feet. These designations are of very little value to the purchaser because they do not tell him the length of the rod while it is in motion under bending stress. That is when it achieves its casting length. This can be determined only under full line load at the moment of greatest bend in the act of casting. The measured chord that subtends the arc of the fully bent rod becomes the true casting or effective length. Accordingly, a nine-foot rod, under full bend, may become a seven-foot rod. Another nine-foot rod, stiffer than the first nine-footer, may be eight feet in length. Or to put it another way, a stiff seven-footer may be effectively longer than a limber nine-footer. All this is not merely academic. It has a very practical application on every cast that is made. It determines, for example, how much line the caster can pick up or retrieve for the backcast. It determines whether or not he can hold a backcast above the weeds or obstructions behind him. It tells him, on a forward overhead cast, the most accurate of all, whether or not the line and leader will clear his head or catch him in the back of the neck; or if he must resort to a sidearm cast, the least accurate of all casts, in order to avoid a distressing collision.

For me, effective length is a very serious matter. In much of my meadow stream fishing, it is often necessary to kneel or even to lie fully prone on one side to avoid spooking a nervous

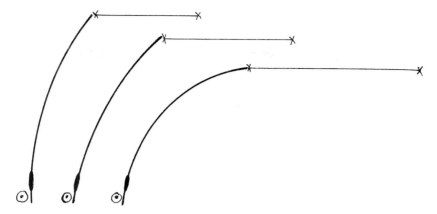

Rods get shorter, backcast lower, with progressive and butt-action tapers as the cast gets longer.

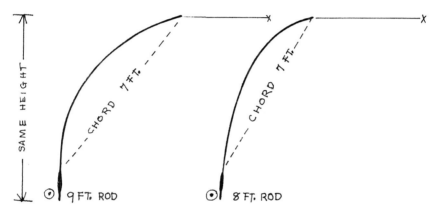

Stiffer, lighter eight-footer—same casting length as softer, heavier nine-footer with same line load.

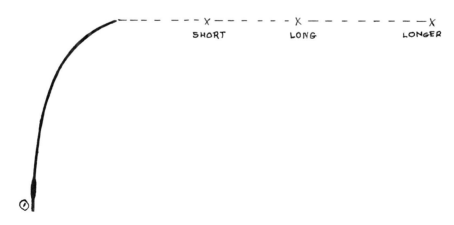

Backcast remains relatively high with tip-action rods, no matter what the length of the cast.

trout. A cast under those circumstances, especially a long one, needs an effective length that will hold the cast well above-ground.

Today the mania for very short rods has aggravated the problem of obtaining adequate casting length. We have been oversold on the short rod. The common spectacle of the short-rod fisherman reaching mightily heavenward to get a higher backcast represents an admission that he needs more length.

In the proper circumstances short rods are delightful to use. I have built many of them and still use them but only where they are suited to the circumstance as on wide shallow rivers where I can wade and have lots of room in front and behind or on small brushy streams where maneuverability is important. They are a very poor choice for open meadow waters where the use of anything under seven and a half feet makes me unhappy. It was with great reluctance that I abandoned the longer rods in my early days of rod-building—rods of nine feet or more. Length begets bulk and weight if the rod is to be made stiff enough for good casting but long rods tire, drain energy, and lack the delicacy of delivery needed for short casts. And yet I never quite gave up the desire for the long rod if only I could have it light and stiff and sensitive. I used to dream of a dry-fly rod—nine feet long, weighing under four ounces. It is a will-o'-the-wisp that I have chased for many years. The solution came about in an interesting way. In my early days of rod-building I floundered about a great deal until I made the acquaintance of the late Robert Crompton, a professional rod-builder from Saint Paul, Minnesota. He was a kindly and sympathetic man who helped me overcome many difficulties. I owe him a great debt for that early guidance. As a matter of fact, I think that there are other rod-builders who owe him the same kind of debt. That brings me to a consideration of the third important step, namely, the designing of rods in profile.

Crompton used to insist over and over again that no rod is fit to be a casting tool if it is made with a straight taper. All those long early weepy rods were made with straight tapers. He declared that only convex tapers would make a good rod. The convex taper is obtained by swelling the diameter of the straight taper without changing the diameters at the ends of the joint. Following Crompton's dictum, a great many rods with convex tapers were put on the market by one manufacturer back in the early 1930s. I examined them carefully and found them to be very disappointing. They were, indeed, very stiff but clubby in the hand and lacked the sensitivity needed for short casts. Eventually they went off the market. In the light of my own experience in later years I found that the mistake lay in the bad management of both the diameters and the convex tapers.

Convex tapers are not a new thing. They originated thousands of years ago in man's early architecture and were used principally as an aesthetic device to satisfy the eye in viewing the columns of temples. A convex taper looks straight. A straight taper does not. Later the convex principle was applied to ships' masts to stiffen them against excessive bending. Today it is used often in the barreled arrow shafts of the archer in order to spine them for heavier bows, while retaining the small diameter and lighter weight. For many years I experimented a great deal with convex tapers and made some very good rods. But I was always obsessed with the idea of getting more length. I still wanted that nine-footer.

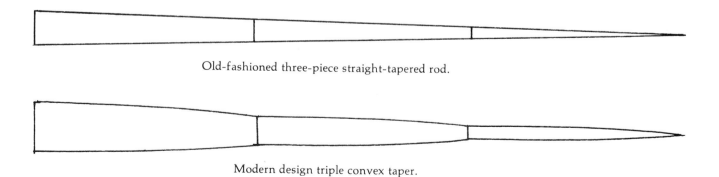

Old-fashioned three-piece straight-tapered rod.

Modern design triple convex taper.

In my experiments I found that there are widely differing results in the use of convex tapers, depending on where the peak of the swell is placed in the joint. It can be placed in the butt end, in the middle, or near the small end as in sketches 2, 3, and 4. The application of these variations depends largely on the kind of action that the caster wants. Rod action is a very loosely defined term and is expressed in many ways, but I think that it finally resolves itself as a matter of where you want the rod to bend. This is very important. Without some bend in the rod the ordinary caster cannot sense or does not have time to sense the change in directions in the act of casting. With an ultra-stiff rod, timing the change of directions and "keeping the line alive in the air," as the tournament casters say, are impossible for the ordinary citizen. If you start the forward cast a millisecond too soon, the momentum is lost and the cast dies; too late and the cast expires behind you. The ultrastiff rod belongs on the casting platform in the hands of those few geniuses who know how to handle it and even they must not dally or bobble about in delivering the cast. It must be done in something like four finely timed strokes in the distance shoot.

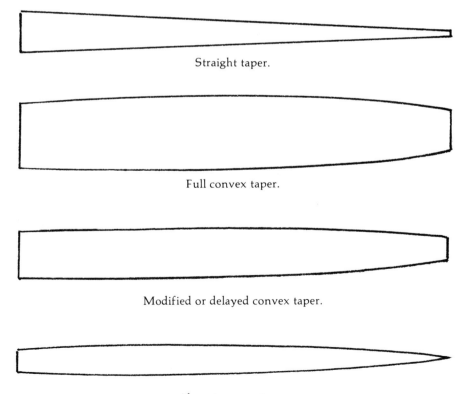

Straight taper.

Full convex taper.

Modified or delayed convex taper.

Abrupt convex taper.

All profiles shown here are somewhat exaggerated.

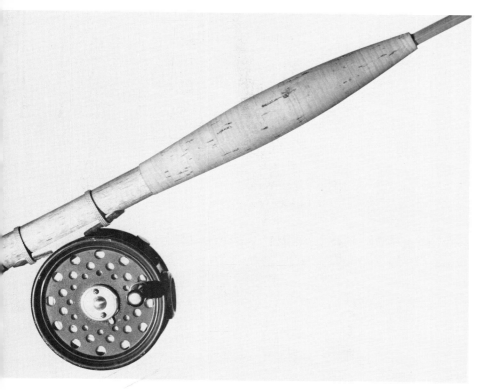

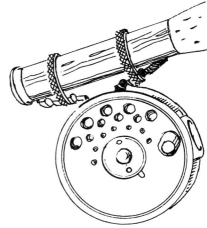

The butt end of the rod should be kept as lightly burdened as possible. This combination of cork, high-density balsa wood, and small springy reel-seat rings (which can be pinched and slid over the reel foot, then released to tighten into one of the crossgrooves of the reel foot) makes a lighter and more secure arrangement than a screw lock, which either unscrews itself or often requires a wrench to unscrew it. The grooved reel foot shown is the old Hardy Brothers design—a good one!

The kind of rod I am discussing is the kind that would be used by the vast majority of fishermen. I exempt salmon, steelhead, and saltwater fishermen. My prescription calls for a rod of adequate casting length, light in the hand, allowing great delicacy of delivery on short casts, and with enough backbone to make a punch shot, accurately out from fifty to sixty feet. Note that I am not talking about the legendary ninety- to one-hundred-foot casts. The number of people who can throw just sixty feet accurately or inaccurately belong to a regal minority. Even in tournament dry-fly accuracy contests, over a long history comparatively few have ever made a first round perfect score, perhaps twenty individuals among all those superb casters. That furthest target, a thirty-inch ring out at only fifty feet, is the one that has ruined many a fine score. But accuracy, we must have—accuracy on the order of a few inches leeway, and if the right kind of rod will help us to get it, then that is the kind of rod we must have.

The rod that I am prescribing is a large order. It is the most difficult of all rods to build for it represents a great bundle of compromises.

I cannot recall in my rod-building of having overlooked any known kind of action, all the way from parabolic to the old tip-action dry-fly tournament type. I had and still have a great fondness for the tip-action type. It has the greatest effective or casting length because it is stiff for two-thirds of its length, permitting a high backcast. It is inherently more accurate than any other type. I found, however, that the tips broke down very quickly, needing replacement often. The butt action or parabolics with their thick clubby tips were not suitable for my purpose. These rods are popular for saltwater use where long slow casts must be used with no great requirement for delicacy. No one fishes size 24 midges in salt water. Moreover, they are not capable of the kind of accuracy needed in my fishing where oftentimes the deviation of a few inches is fatal.

I have the same objections to the progressive taper where the bending starts near the hand and gradually increases toward the tip.

All rods weave more or less in the act of casting, caused principally by a twisting of the casting hand. Right hands twist the rod clockwise. Left hands twist counterclockwise. If you use a rod with loose ferrules, you will eventually find the guides corkscrewed around the rod. It can be overcome by only the most rigid self-discipline. Parabolic and progressive tapers magnify this weave, enlarging the horizontal travel of the weave from side to side because the weave starts closer to the hand.

The error is enlarged geometrically with the extension of the cast.

The rod I wanted has the virtues of the dry-fly tip-action rod plus the durability of the parabolic and the progressive tapers. The latter are more durable because the bend is spread out over a greater length. I am partial to three-piece rods not only because of portability but because I have better control of the tapers in manufacture. The butt joint of my projected nine-footer was no problem. I wanted it stiff enough to confine the action in the upper regions. I employed, therefore, the full convex in sketch 2. The middle joint where most of the bend would take place needed a modified or delayed convex as in sketch 3. The desired effect here was to soften and spread the bend over a greater area than the fragile tip-action dry-fly rod. The top joint needed refinement for delicacy in short casts, plus some stiffening from the convex design to prevent excessive fallover on long casts (see sketch 4).

If you look at sketches 2, 3, and 4, you will note subtle differences. Sketch 2 is a full convex with the peak of the swell in the central region of the joint. This provides the stiffest kind of joint. Sketch 3 is somewhat flattened in the central region with the peak of the swell moved toward the smaller end of the joint. This joint allows more bend than number 2. Sketch 4 shows a joint with the peak of the swell near the thick end and its influence is carried forward more gradually toward an extremely fine point.

This is the most interesting variation of all because it solved the problem of combining delicacy and limited bend in the tip joint. The top half of the top joint is the most critical area in any rod. It is the part that delivers the final impulse or thrust that determines the character of the cast. I have agonized longer and more often over the construction of that last one or one and a half feet of rod than any other part. The great blessing of the convex design lies in the possibility of controlling the amount of bend or tip fallover so that it remains just about the same on short weak casts as with the powerful thrust of a long cast. This control is not possible with straight tapers.

Straight tapers are especially bad on long casts. If they are refined for delicacy, they buckle downward and pile the line and leader in front of the caster before they can reach the target.

Any one of the convex joints that I have designed and shown in sketches 2, 3, and 4, by itself, would not make a good rod. All of them together or in combination make a superb rod. That is the way I got my nine-foot dry-fly rod, weighing less than four ounces.

One final thought. In the special world of the people who work artfully in marble, there is often used a very beautiful and reverent expression to describe this fine material. It is called *pietra serena*, "the serene stone." Even so, bamboo!

Part Two

ADVENTURES
WITH
SPECIAL
FLY
PATTERNS

Chapter Five

A Game of Nods

THERE IS AN OLDER GENERATION OF FISHERMEN, TO WHICH I BELONG, who have memories of a special kind of pleasure, not evident today. Those memories belong to the days of pure silk lines and silkworm gut leaders, when preparations for a day's fishing involved a special kind of ritual, religiously observed. The day always began with the stretching, cleaning, and greasing of the pure silk lines that would not float well, undressed. Then came the sorting and examining of the silkworm gut leaders to choose one suitable for the conditions of that day and perhaps to add a new tippet or two, after which the leader needed to be soaked and softened for a considerable length of time to make it pliant.

All this required some time and a satisfactory location. There was such a place, on the bank, beside the Letort—a lovely, grassy sun-drenched spot, lush and soft to sit upon—and there I went at the beginning of each fishing day to prepare my tackle in the many little ways now cherished only in memory.

Close to the bank where I sat, and just a little off the main current, there was a little eddy that caught much of the flotsam coming downriver and held it interminably while it spun around very slowly. That was an interesting eddy, because in it lived an interesting trout.

I became aware of him one fine summer morning while I was in the midst of preparing my tackle and, as always, with one eye on the river. There was that tiny little bulge in the surface film, a faint dividing of the current and a little circular ripple expiring with the flow of the quiet water. I saw it out of the corner of an eye, my fringe vision if you please, which no fly-fisherman should neglect to cultivate assiduously.

The next time he rose I was prepared for him so that I was able to see and locate his home and his riseform. I did not know it at the time but this trout had a name. In fact, I myself christened him and called him "the Untouchable." But this happened a long time afterward, when I had made many hundreds of casts and had suffered as many refusals.

At first it was a very friendly contest. Even so, his refusals astonished me a little. I rationalized my failures with the thought that I was not really trying to catch him. Anyway, he was a likable fellow. I did not want to discourage his presence in the eddy and I wanted him to be a part of my little ceremony of preparation on the soft grassy, sun-drenched bank near his home. I continued to make my futile casts to him; then, upon being refused, I tipped the long bill of my fishing cap in a silent tribute to his shrewdness and went my way to seek a more gullible breed of trout.

Eventually the contest began to take on a grimmer aspect and with it, finally, came the somber realization that this trout could not be taken, not by me. On the morning of that realization the well-prepared tackle was laid aside, and I made no more casts, for now I had to watch his every move and discover, perhaps, why he defeated me and why I had failed. He had humbled me, this trout of the eddy. His refusals were as eloquent as the spoken word. So began my long vigil while the trout of the eddy continued to flirt his tail, and make his darting upward rises entirely unconcerned with my resentment and my watchful waiting.

Then, bit by bit his way of life was revealed to me. There was no blinding flash of revelation. There were only bits and scraps of information to be sorted and related and evaluated. There was, however, one outstanding fact to be considered more than anything else. He turned out to be an individualist, a kind of gourmet among trout, because this trout ate only one kind of insect, which he, invariably, chose among the many displayed for his pleasure on the traveling dinner table near his eddy. What was this one insect? Was it one of the breed of aristocratic mayflies to which all trout are extraordinarily addicted? Or was it one of the bourgeois family of terrestrials born and bred in the rich meadows bordering the Letort? No, it was none of these. It was, of all things, the common housefly!

He ate them in enormous quantities, all day long, day after

day. Their presence on the water in large numbers was a bit of a mystery until I traced the fly-bearing current upstream to the most obvious housefly source in all the world—namely, the dung heaps of a barnyard on the bank adjacent to the water. There was a convenient watering place too, where cattle were accustomed to linger, switching contentedly at houseflies during the hot summer days. A housefly is not to be scorned because of these associations. After all, he must and should rank with mushrooms and other delectable gourmet foods with a similar lowly origin.

It was plain then that I must cause the downfall of the trout in the eddy with an imitation of the housefly. Nothing else would do! So, I tied houseflies and houseflies. I made many casts with those flies and continued to get nothing but refusals. My most artful imitations were of no avail and even a few secret incantations, supplementing my casts and practiced only in dire emergencies, amounted to nothing but idle gestures.

Again the well-prepared tackle was laid aside and again I watched this fellow more intently than ever before, but now I saw something new to consider. The trout in the eddy did not eat all the houseflies that paraded before him. Many were taken, it is true, but many were rejected even after the most careful inspection in that manner peculiar to a trout—his nose barely touching the insect, undulating backward with the current, frowning-frowning, finally accepting or rejecting the offering as it pleased him.

Now I knew that the trout in the eddy must be ignored; instead, the housefly must be watched to discover why it was often rejected by the trout. A housefly is a very interesting creature. He has some unusual gifts and habits. Aerodynamically, he is some kind of an oddity—a biological freak. He isn't supposed to be able to do the things that he can do. The laws of inertia were certainly not made for him. From a standing start without any visible windup he can take off with blinding speed without the need for gradual acceleration. It is a mystery why houseflies do not leave their wings behind, torn from their bodies, by the terrific counterforces generated by that amazing takeoff. Moreover, he lands the same way. It is very difficult to follow him in flight; only when he is hovering or buzzing in tight little circles can we see him well. He also has another odd characteristic: he can remain absolutely immobile and lifeless in appearance like a "painted fly on a painted river," to paraphrase a famous quote.

Finally, in desperation, as the last measure of my resources, I began to play a game of nods. It is something that I invented many years ago. In those days when all the logical steps had been taken, when my reasoning, inductive or deductive, failed to achieve a successful dry-fly imitation, the game of nods was the last resort. The game is played by tying a reasonable facsimile of the insect being taken by the trout. Then many variations of this basic pattern are tied with only slight differences in each of them. These are in turn cast to a visible feeding trout, and his reaction noted very carefully. A trout has different ways of showing his interest in a fly. He may, when the fly is seen, suddenly begin to accelerate his fins, lifting his head for a brief instant, then suddenly drop to his original position. Or, if the fly is cast to the right or left of the trout, he may nod sideways, briefly toward the fly indicating his interest. Or, if his interest is really aroused, the nod may become a leisurely movement that puts him under the fly to drift with it and inspect it very carefully. Each fly is cast as long as it receives a nod from the trout. When it no longer excites any nods it is discarded for a new variation, each of them being rated for the number of nods. At the end of the game all the highest rated variations are combined into one desirable and perhaps successful pattern.

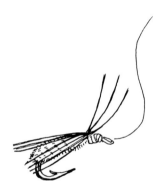

It was in this fashion that I played the game of nods with the trout of the eddy and finally, one late summer day, my efforts were rewarded. He slid under one of my housefly patterns, put his nose under it and drifted backward with it, frowning-frowning, while I trembled a little from the realization that free float was about to end and drag begin. Suddenly he made up his mind, lifted and sucked the fly. Exultant, I lifted the rod tip, felt the resistance for a moment, then it was gone and the fly popped out of the water to drift aimlessly along the ground. I had a brief glimpse of the trout streaking away for cover. At times like this it is best to just sit quietly for a while, to just stare at things—the sky, the water, trees, flowers—and have no serious thoughts of any kind. The hiatus, occupied by his reverie, will prepare the fisherman for a calm appraisal and judicious thought. So I came out of my own reverie, picked up the successful fly, and looked at it very carefully. It had a thin body of unstripped peacock quill and a wing made by tying pale bluish hackle fibers flat over the body and clipped at the rear to make a flat glassy wing like the housefly has at rest. There was something else. At the head of the fly there were three long glinting alert looking hackle fibers and as I stared at these the light of understanding began to glimmer and glow, faintly at first, then with increasing brilliance. I knew now why some houseflies were taken and some were rejected. I lifted the fly toward my lips and I blew gently on the fibers—blew from the sides, blew rear and front. I blew from above and below. Then I put the fly in the palm of my hand and rocked it gently and with every puff of wind, every little rock, the three glassy alert fibers trembled and nodded and quivered to resemble the only movement I had forgotten in the housefly's catalog of characteristics, namely, his ancient habit, no matter how still or lifeless he may appear to be of lifting and rubbing together his two forefeet! This was the sign that the trout of the eddy looked for. From that day forward all my houseflies wore antennae, never fewer than two, never more than three.

In the succeeding years, the housefly incident acquired an increasingly greater significance in my mind, particularly because it gave me a new approach in appraising the efficacy of fly patterns.

I continued to play the game of nods and in doing so came to appreciate those occasions when a particular pattern would bring a trout up to make a repeated inspection. When you have done that much you have gone a long way in devising a successful imitation and you are very close to the secret of what imitation really is.

I did not confine myself to my own patterns in playing this game but went further to review and reevaluate the appeal of many famous older patterns. Some of them certainly are justified in their existence and their fame. Among these the old Red Quill dry fly, often described as "the dry-fly man's sheet anchor," is one of the best and deserves its fame. This is the recipe for this fine old pattern:

> *Body:*   stripped peacock herl undyed from the eye. feather—with pronounced light and dark banded markings.
> *Hackle:*   bright red cock hackle.
> *Wings:*   pale or medium starling primary feather.
> *Tails:*   a few fibers of red cock spade feather.

In the variations that I have used I found that a dark mahogany red hackle was a poor choice; bright red hackle is best, and I found, exactly as A. Courtney Williams states, that it is a very successful pattern for "bulging" or "tailing" fish. It is at its very best in small sizes 18 to 24 and very deadly on the quiet, smooth surfaced waters.

Another exceptionally good pattern comes from Frederic Halford's first book. It is described as a male black gnat. The wings are palest starling primary. The body is made from the black quill of a chaffinch tail feather. This is unobtainable but I have used stripped peacock quill from the eye with success. I do not believe that the body matters at all. The hackle is important. It comes from the shoulder and throat of a cock starling—an extremely short, narrow hackle with a blue black metallic sheen,

which is very difficult to describe. Use two of them. Tails are a few black fibers from a rooster neck or spade hackle. By far the best sizes are 20 to 24.

This is one of the deadliest flies in existence. I have had some marvelous days with this pattern, mind-blowing days when one good fish after another was raised and hooked: days when the excitement was so intense that the breathing came hard and the mouth got dry. Those are the days, infrequent to be sure, when a trout fisherman really finds out why he is out on a trout stream.

Note well, in the above patterns, the use of starling feathers. This is a plentiful bird, and a nuisance that is almost impossible to eradicate. It is a pity that Americans are almost completely unfamiliar with this bird as a source of fly-tying material. The British have for hundreds of years prized this bird highly as a source of fine fly-tying material. Skues once exclaimed in admiration that a starling wing feather was so fine and transparent that he could read his newspaper through one of them.

In these days of diminishing sources of natural fly-tying materials, this bird can furnish an unfailing supply of very useful feathers. In the early days of fly-tying history it was called a stare or shepstare and now a starling. The vast numbers of these birds in America are primarily of Russian stock. The old English starling, according to some opinion, had more vivid coloring, particularly a greater distribution of the bottle green hackles even to the top of the head and once so highly prized for certain patterns. From this bird came the hackle, a blue black body feather, for W. C. Stewart's most famous wet fly, the Black Spider. Stewart was a market fisherman. He and his family depended heavily on his success as a trout fisherman for their livelihood. He would, therefore, want to use the most killing fly available. The Black Spider was his choice along with two others.

The late James Leisenring, Pennsylvania's famed wet-fly artist, also a market fisherman, liked this fly very much and relied

SMALL STARLING
HACKLE ¾ INCH LONG
FOR TINY DRY FLIES

on it a great deal. Inside the wing of the starling are found more of the very desirable feathers used for wet flies. These are soft dun-colored feathers with a gold-colored band all around their edges. This is the best hackle substitute for the once-famed dotterel wet fly. The English dotterel bird was so much sought by English tiers that it became almost extinct. It became a protected bird under law and is no longer available. I never had but a few of these feathers, which were found in an ancient English fly book. These were body feathers used as hackle with that same golden band around the edge as I have described for the starling inside wing feather. The remainder of this dotterel feather is colored a soft creamy tan, once described by Skues as cream-in-the-coffee color. The starling feather has the same mobile quality of the dotterel that ensures "good play" in the water.

It is generally recommended that starlings be collected in early winter when the birds are full-feathered and when fiber cohesion is at its best for wing purposes, but I have found that birds collected in late summer are satisfactory, especially because light-colored wing feathers are obtainable at this time before they have darkened with the fall and winter hue. The older cock starling is, of course, the most desirable. He will have the best developed hackle.

This is not an easy bird to collect. He is wary and knows how to avoid traps. He is also one of the worst pillagers I have ever seen. I have had to watch, helpless with rage, when they stormed into my cherry trees, in big flocks, growling and snapping and defying me. I tried in many ways to discourage them but could not prevent them from completely denuding the trees of all fruit. Eventually, I obtained a short-range pellet gun with which I mollified my outraged feelings by collecting a good supply of very useful feathers.

Another excellent pattern, and this time one that is strictly an American invention, is the Adams. It had its origin in Michigan, allegedly to imitate the numerous caddis hatches or sedge flies as the British call them. This one is outstanding in its appeal to the trout in all sizes. I have used it exclusively in small sizes for my limestone fishing. It has the squatty, low profile appearance that works so well during the terrestrial fishing season when most insects are low-riding in the surface film of the water. This too works well in all sizes but I prefer the small sizes, 20 to 24.

The next pattern in review is one of my own; I have relied heavily upon it for years. It was never tied by me to represent any specific insect but it serves admirably well as a general imitation of the numerous small terrestrials in midsummer. I would never be without this one in my box.

The principal ingredient in the recipe for this pattern comes from the blue black toppy feather of the American wood duck. Two or three of these slender, delicate feathers are twisted together to form a short piece of yarn, which is then used to form the body. The hackle is composed of a few turns of light blue dun and a few of the same fibers for tails. There is no conventional wing. It is best only in small sizes, 20 to 24. It sounds simple, doesn't it? But that is often the way with the best and deadliest of patterns. It should be tied sparsely in order to present it in the surface film.

I have often pondered about the reason for this fly's effectiveness and I feel sure now that when the fly is cast into the film those extremely fine ends of the scarfed toppy feathers become playful in the water and create the illusion of life, so becoming more enticing to the trout.

In recent years, all flytiers and fishermen have become more and more restricted in the choice of natural materials for fly-tying. The current ban on importation and use of jungle cock is an example of this. This is one of the great feathers of all time. It is hard for me to imagine jassids and beetles without it, not to mention the distress of salmon flytiers who can no longer tie the traditional patterns to include this beautiful feather. Many of us are now casting about looking for substitutes with which we can make and use the same patterns and, hopefully, with the same success.

The substitute that I shall now describe turned out so well that I must include it as a regular pattern in my fly box. The principal feather comes from the golden pheasant neck feathers. The small tippet feathers near the top of the neck are useful for our purpose. Even better are the short broad feathers at the base of the neck below the orange cape tippets. These are usually a metallic green and in some birds there are often red and buff-colored ones. All are short, broad, stiff feathers requiring no lacquer to hold and keep their shapes. Two of these feathers, even of different colors, can be laid one on top of another, to form the back of a fine beetle pattern. Golden pheasant is, of course, a commercially raised breed and will always be available.

There is another method, perhaps the most versatile of all that I have seen and like very much, for beetle and jassid ties. Once when I had a meeting with the late Joe Brooks after his return from Tasmania he handed me several very intriguing patterns tied and sent to me by an Australian friend of his, David Scholes. The backs of his beetles and jassids were formed by using small whole feathers, first stripping them to the required size, then tying them in at the neck of the fly by the soft end of the feather, not the hard quill end. It is absolutely ingenious and suggests unlimited possibilities.

Perhaps the most remarkable fly of recent invention is the cricket, which had its origin in the Pennsylvania limestone country. It is regarded by many as the most killing fly of modern times.

As a general purpose fly it is unexcelled for it will raise trout that are in position to feed with amazing regularity even though there are no insects on the water. It is presumably an imitation of a terrestrial, but its enormous appeal to the trout is a mystery for the simple reason that the cricket, even though it flourishes in abundance in the meadows, is rarely found on the water. It is especially attractive to very large trout, with a history of many taken on it up to ten pounds. It is probably the most popular

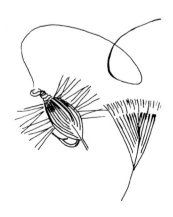

fly in the limestone country today. I am continually astonished
by the fact that the most killing flies in fly-fishing history are
of very simple composition. That is true of this one. There are
some variations but the usual tie is nothing more than a rather
plump body of dark spun fur (brown or mink-colored is fa-
vored) and a wing of black-dyed deer body-hair—nothing else.
It is fished strictly as a dry fly, usually in sizes 14 and 16.

The Spinner: The Unfinished Fly

American fly-fishermen have long denied themselves the
pleasure and satisfaction of fishing to the frenzied rises during a
heavy fall of spinners. For many years in writing and in speech
I have tried to alter this attitude. It is some satisfaction to me
that many fishermen have now adopted my views and no
longer ignore this wonderful phase of fly-fishing. It can be a
glorious experience.

There seems to be some notion that trout do not eat spinners
and are, therefore, not worth imitating. Certainly the British
never made this mistake. In the books of Halford, J. W. Dunne,
and numerous others, including modern British authors, the
spinner is just as highly esteemed as the dun in fishing practice.
And the idea that a spinner is not worth eating is erroneous.
The dying or dead spinner, even though devoid of eggs and the
consequent loss of fats, is nevertheless good eating because the
remaining chitinous structure is solid protein material. Who
would want to deprive himself of the fabulous fishing to the
spinner of the little *Caenis* species *Trichorythodes stygiatus,* or
the fishing during the blizzard-like appearance of the white fly,
Ephoron leukon on the Yellow Breeches, now familiar to many
fishermen? This one is a good case where the dun fishing is
absolutely worthless because the nymphs migrate to the edge of
the bank, where they hatch into the dun and are not thereafter
seen floating on the water. The only fishing to *Ephoron* comes

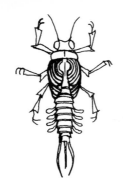

Backpacking nymph with two wing packs.

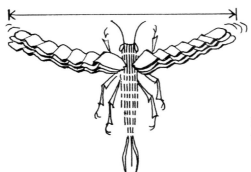

Expansion of the transverse pleats to give the wing its length.

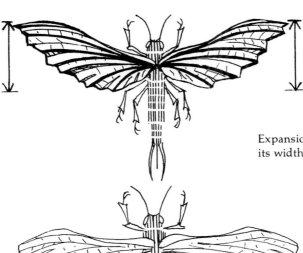

Expansion of the linear pleats to give the wing its width.

Fully opened.

The nymph is a backpacker. In fact, he carries two packs on his back. These are the densely compacted dimensions of his wings. The compacted wings are not viable until he is ready to emerge; then, in a brief flashing instant they are suffused with blood that blows them open to full size. The wings are not folded in those amazing backpacks; they are pleated like an accordion or camera bellows but more amazingly they are pleated in two directions, transverse and linear. The transverse pleats open first and give the wing its full length. Then the linear pleats open to give the wing its width. The transverse pleats seem to disappear but the linear pleats remain sharply indented to create the surprising condenser effect shown in the color photograph of the fallen spinner. The brilliant condenser effect is most pronounced when the spinner first falls flat to the surface of the water. As the spinner becomes more sodden and waterlogged, the condenser effect gradually disappears and is eliminated entirely when disintegration occurs. The artificial spinner tied in the manner I have indicated is the deadliest I have ever used.

when the spinner returns to the water in late evening. This is one female dun, by the way, which does not molt but retains the same covering in the spinner stage when it returns to the water to spin and die. There is no translucency worth mentioning in dun and spinner; it is a dull egg white color and no special effort should be spent to obtain translucency in the imitation. Another oddity about this insect is the fact that the male has two tails whereas the female has three tails.

In *A Modern Dry-Fly Code* I offered a possible solution to the problem of imitating the spinner when I suggested the use of porcupine quill. This is the only material that comes closest to imitating the exact nature of a spinner body. The porcupine quill is also a protein material perfectly matching the spinner body in texture, conformation, and translucency. The method or the material never became popular, probably because it is a little troublesome to manage, but surely it is a far simpler technique than other methods involving the process of making complicated extended bodies. I cannot deny, however, that a simpler, less involved method is more desirable, but I could not abandon the porcupine quill entirely for I still do not know a better way to get a good floating spinner in the very large sizes such as for the big eastern green drake or the huge Michigan *Hexagenia limbata.*

For the body of smaller mayflies the reappearance of seal's fur is certainly a great boon in the tying of spinners—if it is handled correctly.

I think that it is some kind of a minor crime to pollute this superb material by mixing and blending it with other materials. If maximum translucency is desired, it should be used alone and furthermore should never be dubbed on by scarfing or rolling around the tying thread. That simply makes it a dull lifeless material like many others. The only correct method of using seal's fur to the best advantage is to use the Rube Cross method of making a chenille by spreading a pinch or two of seal's fur on a piece of waxed thread after which the thread is doubled back on itself and twisted to form the chenille. The chenille is tied in at the tail and brought forward to form a body and thorax around the wings. The result is an exceedingly rough and shapeless thing that should be thinned out by plucking and discarding any loose fibers. The last step is to trim the entire mass, avoiding the wings by using a fine pointed scissors to shape the thorax and the tapered body, leaving some fibers extending a trifle along the sides of the body through which the light will pass and illuminate the fly with remarkably good effect. No support hackle for the spinner is used in the usual sense because the outspread fiber wings provide that support without obscuring the body. Now we shall see why I have described my spinner as "The Unfinished Fly."

In my studies with the slant tank I experimented extensively with live and dead spinners on the surface of the water, dropping them on the surface in different areas and in different attitudes. In these experiments I was amazed to see the transformation in the appearance of the wing immediately after the spinner fell to the water. In every instance the wings took on a brilliant translucent aspect with long, clear, colorless streaks that are not apparent in an air view of the spinner. After close inspection and considerable thought on the matter, I discovered that this effect was created by the folds in the wing acting as water traps to form light condensers that gathered light above the surface and transmitted this intensified light to the trout. Older writers and observers who bewailed the difficulty of reproducing the delicate, membranous appearance of the spinner never knew or suspected what the real problem was, in reproducing this wing. The hackle fiber wing was certainly the correct approach but it is no good unless it is given the correct treatment. A successful spinner wing must gather and condense the light exactly as is done by the natural spinner. This cannot be done with hackle points, fish scales, cellophane, or the body feathers of various birds. This can be done only with hackle fiber wings and the stiffer the fiber the better. I do not know who was the first to

A greatly enlarged photograph of a wing of *Ephemerella subvaria*, showing the linear pleats.

use hackle fiber for wings but even this is no better than other materials if used in the traditional way. This wing will be the most successful of all, only if the fibers are fixed to remain *widely separated* from one another. If this is done, the widely separated fibers will trap the water between them and form the long brilliant light condensers just as the natural wing does. This does not happen, of course, until the fly is cast on the water. That is why I have called it "The Unfinished Fly." The fly is not completed until you borrow a little water from the surface every time you make a cast.

The spread or splayed effect for the hackle fiber wing is obtained in two steps. First, the turns of hackle are wound as for a wingless dry fly with the fibers perpendicular to the hook shank, about four or five turns, one in front of another; then the succeeding turns are piled in the center of this group, splitting the fibers apart on each successive turn until all the hackle is used and tied off. In the second step the hackle fibers are divided in two equal parts underneath the hook and the tying thread is used to catch and lift one-half of the fibers to a horizontal plane or even above that by reversing and bringing the thread behind and over the hook. The thread must be drawn gently to lift the fibers else it will slip off.

With a slight tension the thread is now passed underneath the hook where the other half of the fibers are caught and lifted to a horizontal plane or above that, after which the thread is turned over and around the shank one or two turns in the normal direction.

The entire procedure should be repeated once more, then when the final turns are completed the thread is crossed in an X fashion on top of the hook shank to split and fix the two halves on the top side of the hook shank. A tiny drop of cement should be applied to these turns to fix them solidly. The total effect should be a wide flat wing with the fibers firmly separated from one another.

TO TIE A WIDESPREAD FIBER SPINNER WING

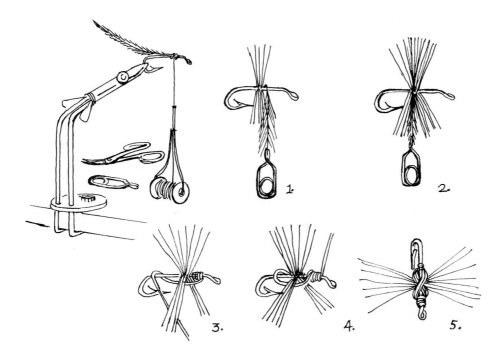

1. Make five or six turns of hackle perpendicular to the hook shank, each turn separated from its neighbor.
2. *Split* the center of the mass with the rest of the hackle and tie off in front. This will spread the hackle fibers.
3. Pick up one-half of the hackle underneath with the thread and reverse the direction of tying by going behind the hackle and over the top of the hook shank.
4. Come forward with the thread and pick up the other half underneath. Pass the thread in the normal direction over the neck of the hook, draw gently to elevate both halves, adjusting to half-spent or full-spent style, then secure with two or three turns around the neck. Repeat this procedure at least once more to firm up the wings.
5. Split the top half of the hackle with figure X turns and tie off.

An easier method of splitting the hackle mass to form the wings is to tie in some thorax material before the hackle is turned. Two pieces of material (such as goosewing fibers, raffia, or peacock herl) are tied in, top and bottom, at the thorax, extending either behind or out beyond the eye. After the fibers are turned, as above, the thorax material is brought back, top and bottom, then tied down behind the wings or in front of the wings. With this method you get only a full-spent tie, not the valuable and killing half-spent obtainable with the first method.

In the Surface Film—An Ethic

"There is no such thing," thundered Frederic Halford from his pulpit in 1913, "as a halfway house between dry- and wet-fly fishing. Either the fly is floating, in which case it is dry-fly fishing or it is more or less submerged and is wet-fly fishing."

I have great admiration for Halford. All of us owe him a considerable debt for his enormous labors expended in improving a fine sport. I am continually fascinated by his character and philosophy and by his puritanical views. As far as his fly-fishing was concerned, he lived on an exalted plane that few, if any, have ever achieved or professed. If there was any way that Halford could have floated his dry flies without touching the surface of the water, he would have done so. There is a spirituality about him and his fishing that comes through in brief flashes now and then. Halford's attitude and influence undoubtedly contributed to the controversy that exploded and raged for a lengthy period between his followers and Skues's followers over the efficacy and propriety of using wet flies and nymphs on the chalk streams, which were regarded by many as the sacred domain of the dry fly. Eventually, the controversy died out and was never revived. Today, if there is such a difference of opinion, it is never expressed in any objectionable way except as a sporting tolerance for one another. Anyway, I think that everyone became dreadfully worn out from hearing the silly argument—like the two Kilkenny cats that fought so long until nothing but their tails were left.

Viewed objectively, in the cold light that prevails with the passage of time and the remoteness of that ancient controversy, I think that we can fairly say that Frederic Halford, Grand Sachem of the dry fly, stood for a *way to fish*, whereas Skues, Grand Vizier of the wet fly and a dry-fly fisherman too, stood for a *way to catch more fish*. I make no judgment here on the ethics or virtuosity of each man's position. But in appraising Halford's position I find, in the religiosity of his attitude, an overly severe restriction on his own pleasure and fishing opportunities for I think that the dry fly has a far wider application in practice than Halford allowed himself to believe.

We must begin with the proposition that no matter how dry the fly is, it must touch the water and be exposed to the air at the same time. If this idea is carried out to its logical conclusion, all of us must agree that if the smallest portion is exposed to the air no matter how deeply submerged the fly may be, it is still a legitimate form of the dry fly. Thus, I can in good conscience include in a true dry-fly category an emerger pattern that has broken through the surface film and is only minutely exposed to the air. I can, of course, also include anything lying between these two extremes, such as spinners and low-floating terrestrials. Thus, I would have urged upon Frederic Halford a reconsideration of his narrow view in order to include any fly, natural or artificial, touching the surface film whether it be on the film, in the film, or mostly under the film. Those separations, effected by an interface that distinguishes them by only a faint micrometer's breadth from one another, are, nevertheless, worlds apart in appearance and behavior to the trout as we have seen from our studies of the slant tank.

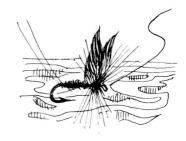

Heretofore I have been largely concerned with appearances on the film and in the film with only an occasional venture into that area under the film. One of my adventures with the underside of the interface was purely accidental. I have previously explained how I played the game of nods with many artificials, new and old. One of the old ones that occupied my attention was the Greenwell's Glory, often nominated by many respected British authors as the greatest wet fly of all time and a fly so famous that it has become a familiar byword to nonfishermen as well as fishermen. Any fly with those distinctions should not be ignored by anyone. It earned its reputation chiefly as a wet fly but is also distinguished as a dry fly. In a recent British publication I saw a photograph of an original authenticated Greenwell's Glory tied by the originator James Wright and now in the possession of the Flyfishers Club of London. I was immensely impressed by the fact that it was tied in the same manner as a dry fly, with upright wing and hackle, not slanting backward as for a wet fly. Seemingly, it violates the tenets of good entry and good play as required for wet flies. In view of its outstanding notoriety as a wet fly, the manner of tying apparently did not matter.

I tied the Greenwell as a dry fly, adding some tail fibers that the original did not have. I did not have English blackbird for the wing, which is unobtainable in America, so I looked about for a reasonably close substitute and finally settled upon the wing feathers of the European jay, with strange results. Waxed yellow tying silk and gingerish cock-y-bondhu hackle completed the materials for the fly and I proceeded to tie a considerable supply of these in a dry pattern on size 16, finely tempered lightweight hooks that I was fortunate enough to obtain.

I wanted to test the pattern for specific use during the sulphur hatch. I began to use it in the early stage of the hatch with great anticipation and discovered much to my disappointment that it was a very poor floater even though the hook was small and very light and materials apparently the best. I do not ordinarily use flotants for my dry flies, but rely heavily on good quality materials for proper flotation. I could not get but one or two floats with that fly before it became sodden every time thereafter. I began to regret the waste of labor and material expended on those useless dry flies that I could not float even with the most vigorous and frequent false casts. The fly did not sink deeply, barely breaking and hanging in the surface film, and slipping into the water with surprising ease on each cast. I could see it very clearly near the surface. I was about to end my brief experience with this no-good dry fly when I saw a disturbance on the surface that looked like a rise. For a moment I did not connect it with my drifting, very wet dry fly, but when I lifted I found that I was hooked to a trout. I continued to fish with the same fly, putting it over every rise that I saw, and getting a strike on almost every pitch.

HANGING EMERGER

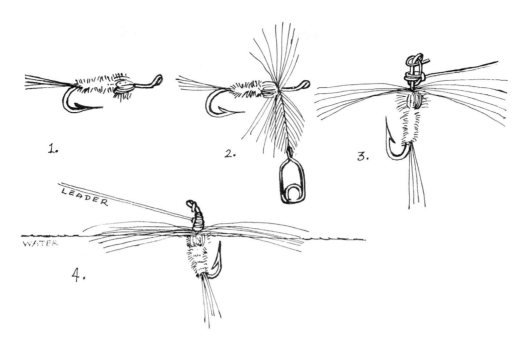

1. Construct a nymph on a long shanked heavy wire hook leaving at least 1/8 inch of neck.
2. Add two turns of a long fibered stiff neck hackle (wattle) close to the thorax. The wattles are found along the edge of all necks.
3. On the remaining portion of the bare neck tie a riffle hitch, which is simply two half hitches added to the neck after the leader has been tied to the eye.
4. A riffle hitch will force nymph to take a position at right angle to the leader and cause it to fall tail first into the water but holding it against the underside of the surface film by the surface support of the widespread spidery hackle.

There was no doubt at all that these fish were taking emerging duns for on numerous occasions I could see the live duns rising from the water, barely escaping the closing jaws of a hungry trout. For something like a week, every day, I continued to fish that soggy dry fly and continued to hook fish after fish until the trout began to take notice of the floating duns, no longer watching for the drifting emerger. I had to abandon my abortive Greenwell and revert back to a winged high-floating pattern in order to take fish again.

Among the older patterns that I tried there was also the Gold-ribbed Hare's Ear, a "no-hackle" pattern of the late 1800s that was often acclaimed the finest of all dry flies. It was so successful that Frederic Halford declared that if he had to choose but one fly, it would be this one. In his later years, while still acknowledging the superiority of this fly, he rejected it entirely because it was not dry enough to suit his narrowing tastes. This fly sinks deeply into the surface film and, like my soggy Greenwell, is undoubtedly a first-rate emerger pattern.

In the aftermath of my curious experience with the Greenwell, I sought and found the reason for its inability to float well. European jay wing feathers are highly water absorbent. They do not repel water like many other feathers. If you plunge one of them into a glass of water, you will find on withdrawal that it is saturated. In the case of many other feathers such as duck or starling, you get only a tiny droplet or two. Additionally, this feather gets very soft and playful in the water. If I were a dedicated wet-fly or nymph fisherman I would be using jay for wings and wing pads.

Following my experiences with these famous patterns, my attention continued to be drawn to the underside of that interface or surface film once aptly described by John McDonald as a "metaphysical border." I wanted above all else to try to duplicate the performance of the nymph touching or clinging to the underside of the surface film with its head exposed and about to emerge. The idea sounds preposterous, I know. Anyway I persisted in my efforts until eventually I came up with the hanging nymph or dangling emerger. Briefly, this is the way it was done. First a suitable hook was chosen; the best for this purpose is a pattern called long-may, a snecky-limerick pattern designed for big mayflies. The wire is rather heavy in the bend, then it tapers very finely to the eye. This is ideal for the hanging nymph because it helps to concentrate the weight near the bend. Any pattern of nymph can be tied on this hook, preferably with water absorbent materials and even the addition of some metal ribbing to make it upset more easily.

The body and thorax should be finished at least 1/8 inch short of the eye. Then the tier should choose one of those very stiff, long-fibered wattles that are found at the edge of a cock's neck. This hackle is tied in and turned only one complete turn with concave or dull side facing the bend. The result is a wide sparse, spidery circle of stiff fibers around the neck. The tie-off should still leave some space at the neck.

The last and very important step is to tie the leader with a turle or some such knot, after which a riffle hitch or two half hitches are made around the neck of the fly. The fly will then be knuckled and standing out at right angles to the leader. The fly should be cast into the air above the water and be given time to upset so that the heavy bend falls and penetrates the surface film. Its descent will be stopped by the large thin spread of stiff hackle resting on the surface and acting as a buoy, allowing only the head to protrude. That is the hanging nymph or emerger.

The peculiar manner in which the nymph effects the contact with the surface film and the eventual emergence is very well explained in *An Angler's Entomology* by J. R. Harris. The water-repellent properties of the ascending nymph combine with the gripping action of the elastic surface film to hold the dangling nymph securely until emergence is completed without any actual contact with the water. I wanted to imitate this same performance with the artificial emerger.

Notes on Dry-Fly Construction

Winged dry flies are still very important to me. There is no substitute for that kind of a dry fly when the trout are concentrating on a hatch of upright-winged floaters. Wing material and wing construction still require better solutions. The cut-hackle wing that I recommended and used for so many years remains a very fine wing; it is durable and shapely and will not turn or spin the fly if it is cut at the soft tip end of the hackle.

Cut wings are absolutely worthless unless they can be cut uniformly so that the pairs are perfectly matched. It was unfortunate that I recommended the cut wing at a time many years ago, when there was a very good wing cutter that went off the market. No one can consistently cut wings freehand and expect them to be perfectly matched. A great deal of dissatisfaction was expressed concerning the cut wing, justifiably so because of the mismatching caused by freehanded cutting. The reappearance of the wing cutter, now on the market again, should render a more satisfactory accounting of this fine wing.

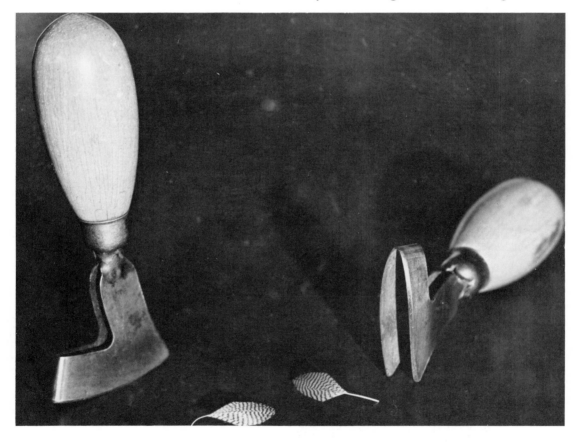

A pair of rocker-type wing-cutters that I have used for the past twenty-five years. I was consulted concerning the shape of the cutting edges about which we had a sharp disagreement. I did not like the marketed pattern with its straight sides and narrow shape. I asked the manufacturer for two untempered blanks that I shaped to suit myself—after which I returned them for tempering and hardening. They have the rounded sides and the wide base to render better the somewhat buxom appearance of the natural wing. Additionally, the cut wing must be broad enough to compensate for the considerable narrowing that takes place when the wings get wet. The two cutters shown are designed for a large fly such as the Green Drake, and a smaller one for medium to small flies.

Alternatively, I have used other winging methods, even some of the older ones. As a matter of fact, I have resorted again to the oldest of them all, namely the matched slip wings from the right and left primary feathers of various birds. It is rare to see this wing anymore because of its tendency to split apart very quickly and lose its shape. Some time ago I took a long, hard look at that old wing and decided that it could be a good wing if handled in a new way.

If you examine old dry flies and older books you can see that when the dry-fly tiers came along, they reversed the flow or curve of the fibers from that of the wet fly. It was a serious mistake, I have to say. To prove this you have only to take a wing feather and hold it by the tip with one hand, then stroke the fibers toward the butt end with the thumb and forefinger of the other hand. The fibers will become completely rent apart and hopelessly disarrayed. If you hold and stroke counterwise, you will find that the fibers remain beautifully composed and the whole feather retains its original symmetry. Fishermen and flytiers, it seems, are the most tradition-bound people on earth. Once a senseless practice has begun it seems to enjoy, unworthily, a long and honorable career. Reversing the flow of the fiber by those early originators of the dry fly was nothing but a disservice to fly-fishermen. You might as well tear the wing apart with your fingers before tying it to your leader. You have only to consider the terrific counterforces working against the grain of the wing, being generated by the act of casting. I am reasonably sure that these forces cause the upright wing to bend sharply and lie flat against the body during the blistering speed of its travel back and forth. The slip wing should be put on with the same back flow as the wet fly, then raised upright by drawing it forward with turns of the tying silk behind the wing. This wing can be made even more durable by putting a very tiny drop of cement at the base and a very small dab at the tips in order to ensure the adhesion of the fibers still further while still retaining flexibility.

RIGHT AND LEFT PRIMARY STARLING WING QUILLS

MATCHING SLIPS RIGHT & LEFT FROM PRIMARY WING QUILLS

WIND AGAINST THE GRAIN STANDARD TIE BAD TECHNIQUE

TINY DROP OF CEMENT

WIND WITH THE GRAIN IMPROVED TIE MORE DURABLE

TO TIE A DUN, THORAX STYLE

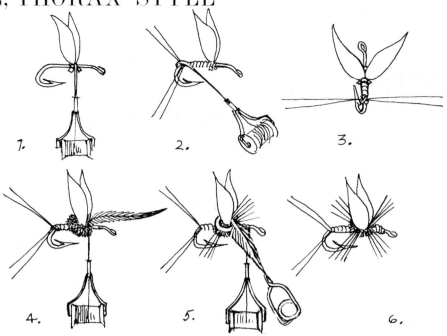

1. Wings in the center of the shank.
2. Run tying silk to rear and tie in tail fibers, splitting them widely apart by tying in only one side at a time. Draw it toward the wings by getting a turn or two of thread behind the fibers and pulling gently. Use one fiber on each side for very small flies, 22^S and 24^S, two fibers on each side for medium flies, 18^S to 22^S, and three fibers on each side for 16^S to 14^S. Place a drop of cement at tails to fix.
3. Tails split widely apart at right angle to hook shank because tails tend to straighten out from repeated pickup.
4. Run thread back to wings; put stem of hackle between wings, dull side down, tie in spun fur yarn. Make a little ball of spun fur around the hook-shank close to the base of the wings. *No body*—just a thorax. The little ball will function as anchoring shoulders to hold the crossed turns of hackle.
5. Tie in hackle with butt fibers long enough to extend slightly past and to cover the bottom of the hook. Angle three complete turns as shown.
6. Reverse the direction of the hackle and angle the turns in the opposite direction at least two turns. One hackle may be enough if it is a long one; otherwise add a smaller, shorter, fibered hackle for the front support.

There is one more invaluable step in the fashioning of this and all other wings. They should be prebroken by simply grasping them with thumb and forefinger, then bending them sharply at the base to make them lie flat against the body, after which they should be raised upright again. In this way they will always bend symmetrically with equal wind resistance in the flight path.

The search for suitable wing material is never ending. A good wing must be soft and flexible, yet it must be firm enough to retain its shape. One of the very best in the slip-wing variety, taken from right and left primary wing quills, comes from the gray goose, either wild or domestic. I know of no other feather with such great adhesion of the individual fibers with one another. It has the other necessary requirements, namely flexibility with firmness. If it is applied with the back-flow position and a bit of cementing, it is practically indestructible. The wild-goose wing quill has one other good use, especially the first primary. On the short side of this feather you will find the finest of all quills for making the bodies of dry or wet flies—far superior to peacock or condor. They are beautifully tapered and have a well-marked segmented effect. What is more interesting is that there is no flue to be removed. These quills can be used by butting the turns against one another on larger flies or over-lapping on smaller flies. It is extremely tough and durable and, of course, it is another plentiful natural material.

Another very good feather for winging dry flies comes from the very common and plentiful ringneck pheasant. They are the small broad feathers at the butt of the wing on the outside. They come, conveniently, in all shades of blue dun from the palest to the darkest. This feather does not have a pronounced curve as do the whole breast feathers of duck that were once so popular for fan-wing dry flies and which were so exasperating in use because they invariably spun around or whirled about no matter how carefully the wings were matched and set. Pheasant wings won't do this. I have rarely had a problem with these wings. I can recommend them without reservation, especially because they have a wonderful range of blue dun coloring.

The thorax style of tie, even though increasingly popular, has not been fully appreciated. In any dry fly requiring very stiff hackle to make it float well, there is a serious problem created by such hackle even though it is desirable; it involves the business of hooking the fish. This is caused by the fact that stiff hackles act as a guard in front of the hook point. (This was never very apparent with large flies and large hooks; but with the increasing and desirable use of small hooks and small flies, that stiff hackle guards the point even more efficiently than ever before, because as the bend narrows and the point gets closer to the shank, the point is guarded by the stiffest portion of the hackle.) The thorax style of tie, with the hackle splayed widely front and rear, eliminates the guard and exposes the point to allow free entry.

In many alleged thorax ties that I have seen, the hackle is tied and turned in the old upright manner, then cut away underneath. This undoubtedly exposes and frees the hook point as with the splayed hackle, except that this method loses a great deal of support for the fly at the critical area near the bend of the hook where all the weight is concentrated. This, of course, necessitates tail support and is a step backward. A true thorax style of tie has part of the hackle slanted backward to cover the bend of the hook and at the same time exposes the point for surer hooking as well as exposing the thorax, which is sometimes visible to the trout. The true thorax tie does not require tail support and, as I explained many years ago in *A Modern Dry-Fly Code*, the tails, widely split, act as governors or outriggers to prevent capsizing of the fly. I note with some amusement that the forked tail idea has been discovered and rediscovered in recent years. The forked tail has indeed been adopted and used with great benefit by many but not forked enough. I wish to emphasize that the tails should be split to give maximum spread, actually at a right angle to the shank of the hook. The reason for this is that repeated pickups of the fly draw the tails backward, thus reducing the spread considerably but allowing enough to remain to keep the fly balanced and properly cocked.

Chapter Six

The Hidden Hatch

I

"THE SMALLEST OF THE MAYFLIES" IS THE WAY THE GENUS *Caenis* IS often described. "The white curse" is another name often applied to it by the British fly-fishermen—and with good reason.

Caenis is the most exasperating as well as the most fascinating of all the insects that trout eat and fly-fishermen try to imitate. It is unique, not only in its tiny size but also in several aspects of its life cycle—aspects that are important to fishermen.

Of all the mayflies, *Caenis* alone completes the metamorphosis from dun to spinner while it is in the air, and often just a

few minutes after hatching from the nymph stage. If you are keen-eyed and observant, you can sometimes see great numbers of spinners still dragging the nymphal shuck as they fly to and fro.

Caenis' entire life and purpose as a winged insect is completed in a single forenoon: It hatches from the nymphal stage, changes from dun to spinner, mates, lays its eggs, and then falls to the water and dies, thus becoming a special attraction to the eager trout.

In both the length of its hatching season and the regularity of its emergence, *Caenis* is the most dependable of the mayflies. From the middle of July until well into October, the tiny insects hatch every morning without fail. On any stream where *Caenis* is well established, the number of hatching insects is enormous.

Caenis is not easy to see, either in the air or on the water. But if your angle of view is just right on any bright morning during *Caenis* season, you will see what appears to be a solid wall of glinting, shining, sunstruck wings extending for twenty feet above the river. The wall will shift and undulate and weave with the vagaries of the air currents.

In the early part of the *Caenis* season the hatch and the resultant rise of trout are of rather short duration, not more than two to three hours. As the season advances, the daily hatch of duns and fall of spinners becomes more and more extensive until it reaches well into noontime, providing some five to six hours of steady fishing.

At the peak of the season the morning cycle of hatching nymphs, molting duns, and falling spinners becomes so heavy that around noon the great mass of spinners becomes compressed near the surface of the water and the insects begin to fall in great numbers. The surface literally becomes carpeted from bank to bank with the dead and dying spinners. If a good stock of trout is in the river, the rise to these dying spinners is really something to see.

Before this last stage, the rise is rather orderly, but on the final massive fall of spinners the trout become frenzied in their eagerness to get as many *Caenis* as possible. They hang close to the surface, shifting back and forth and side to side as rapidly as they can, mouths wide open and slobbering as they gulp gobs of the dying spinners. The habits of *Caenis* and the reaction they cause in trout seem to be the same the world over.

I never see this astonishing performance without thinking of Frank Sawyer, the famous British riverkeeper who made a special study of *Caenis* on the river Avon and described his trout as just staying on the surface gobbling like a duck. I cannot think of a better expression.

How many *Caenis* will one trout get in half a day's feeding? A steadily feeding trout can get 2,000 to 3,000 insects in a single morning.

Autopsies on trout gorged with *Caenis* reveal bulging stomachs and masses of insects lining throat, mouth, and gills. Similar observations are recorded by British fishing writers, who have contended with "the white curse" for many generations. In America there has been no widespread interest in *Caenis* until recent years.

It is really an obscure insect, one of the kind that Charlie Fox likes to call a "hidden hatch." *Caenis* is likely to be ignored, especially where hatches of bigger, showier mayflies are prevalent. The larger hatches are easier to imitate and to fish.

Justin and Fannie Leonard included *Caenis* as one of the important food items for trout in their fine book, *May-flies of Michigan Trout Streams*, published in 1962. It is certainly an important insect on many of our Pennsylvania streams, and is also abundant on New York trout streams.

As you have probably guessed by now, fishing a *Caenis* hatch presents some very unusual problems. The tiny size of the insect is one of them. Tying these minute imitations in sizes 22, 24, and 28 is likely to be a source of despair to many amateur tiers. To me it is old hat because of my long familiarity with the tiny terrestrials. You will surmount this problem if you

feel as I do that there is no finer fishing in the world than dry-fly fishing with tiny artificials and fine gut.

The next serious problem arises from the sheer abundance of insects on the water. Your artificial is competing with so many of the naturals that getting the attention of the trout seems hopeless. You have only to observe how numerous are the naturals that get by him while he is taking just one to realize how serious this problem is.

I have a few rules that I observe religiously to beat these odds, and I offer them with the hope that they will help you too.

First, be on time for the beginning of the morning rise. On the waters that I fish the rise starts between 7 and 8 A.M., daylight saving time. The comparatively sparse display of insects gives you a chance to get a trout's attention. Do not waste your time on a small trout. Pick out a good one, and start working on him immediately.

Second, remain until the very end of the hatch, when all the spinners have been washed away. Often you will find a good trout that is still looking for "just one more."

Third, check minor lines of drift where insects are comparatively sparse. Good trout often occupy side channels and pockets that offer good cover, even though these spots have fewer insects.

Fourth, watch your trout's feeding rhythm. Each trout has a definite feeding pace marked by regular intervals between rises. If you make your pitch out of step with his desire to rise, he will not take your fly. Remember that a trout has little energy reserve compared with warm-blooded animals. Rhythmical feeding is the only way he can profitably use his energy; taking such small insects in any other way would be a metabolic disaster to him.

The only time a trout can break this rhythm profitably is at the end of the spinner fall, when he can down a mouthful of insects at a gulp. Think of it: A trout must move his entire body every time he eats something little bigger than a pinhead, a process that often goes on for many hours. If humans had to eat that way, eating would be dreadfully exhausting.

How big a trout can you hope to take on these tiny flies? To me a twelve- to fourteen-inch trout in good condition taken on *Caenis* and a 7X tippet is a fine achievement. I have taken trout up to eighteen inches long on this tackle. I got three eighteen-inchers in one week during the 1967 season, and two more in 1968. They were all wild, burly, limestone trout.

I have heard of bigger trout being taken on *Caenis* but have never seen them. When I hear such stories I always feel a little ashamed and resolve to do better the next time. My trouble is that someone is always around when I get a good fish, and he always insists on measuring it down to the last fraction. Once in a while I am allowed a quarter-inch leeway just to round out the figures. But seriously, any time I get an eighteen-inch, heavy-bodied wild trout on 7X leader and a No. 22 or 24 hook, I am a proud fisherman, especially if I catch it in weed-choked, log-jammed waters like the Letort.

Technically, one of the eighteen-inchers that I got in 1968 wasn't caught on *Caenis*. Dennis Nawrocki and George Green of Carlisle were fishing with me that morning on the Letort. We caught a few nice trout, and when the hatch and fall of spinners was over we started back toward our cars. On the way back I broke off my No. 24 *Caenis* and put it in my fly box. When I turned for a last look at the water I caught the wink of a rise near a pile of debris. I reached into the fly box and picked out the first thing to hand—a tiny floating ant—and tied it to my 7X leader point.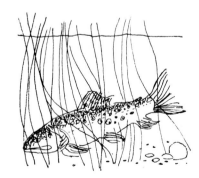

A long downstream float was needed to get the fly over the fish. Two throws went badly. The third was just right, with enough slack in the leader to drift the fly over the trout. As the ant reached the edge of the jam, a long brown shape rose slowly from the cover and sipped the ant in very delicately.

For the next half hour the trout explored every weed bed in

that stretch of water, and I had many apprehensive moments trying to keep my leader free of weed balls and trying to keep the trout from smashing the leader with his tail. Finally, George netted him for me. Though the trout wasn't caught on a complete *Caenis* rig, he *was* caught on 7X leader with a tiny hook during the *Caenis* hatch.

This story has an interesting sequel that points up the great strength of a well-conditioned limestone trout. I have said that trout do not have a great reserve of energy. Even so, for a short while they can exert tremendous power.

After we landed the trout I decided that I wanted to photograph him while he was still alive. First, however, I would have to go home and get my camera. So I put the fish in a cotton-mesh live-bag and put the bag in the water under a bed of watercress. George Green offered to stay and keep an eye on the fish.

While I was gone, George's wife joined him. I returned a short time later, and they met me with somber faces and a tale of woe. While they had been sitting there, they had heard a terrific commotion in the water. They had hurried over to see what it was and had seen my big trout out of the bag and making his way to freedom. I examined the bag and found a big hole in the bottom. Yet, before putting the fish inside I had examined the bag very carefully, even putting my forearm inside and hitting the mesh with my fist. The trout had literally lashed the netting to shreds with his powerful tail.

Now you may ask, why use 7X leader? Why not 6X, which has an enormous margin of strength over 7X? The more experience I have with trout, the more I am convinced that they are not leader-shy—disturbed by the leader's thickness. What disturbs them is a leader that snakes or streaks across the currents. And 7X drags as much as 4X.

I decided long ago that the size of the tippet should be determined by the size of the fly. To behave properly on the surface, size 24 dry flies need 7X tippets. On the other hand, you simply cannot manage the big grasshopper and cricket imitations on such fine leader. You need 3X, 4X, or 5X tippets for such imitations, and plenty of shy trout are caught on those sizes on the Letort and similar waters.

The tiny *Caenis* dun rides the water so lightly that it doesn't even dent the surface film. I can never hope to achieve that kind of performance with the imitation, but I try to get as close to it as possible. A 7X tippet presses the tiny imitation into the surface film less than does a 6X; a 6X presses less than a 5X; and so on.

What about using larger imitations—showing the trout something bigger and different to divert his attention from those ridiculous specks? I have no quarrel with fishermen who believe in this theory, but it has never worked for me. I find that trout are very narrow-minded feeders when a specific hatch is involved.

How do you handle a three-pound trout on such delicate rigging? Can it be done consistently? Certainly, except for those situations where leader of any size is of no avail. There is nothing you can do about a big determined trout that dives into a logjam, wraps the leader around an obstruction, and breaks off without further ceremony. Such incidents have happened to me many times; I hope that they will happen again!

Many years ago when I was working out the now familiar terrestrial patterns (jassids, ants, etc.) in small sizes, I was forced to use very fine natural silkworm gut to make these flies behave properly. In those days fine gut was diamond-drawn to as fine as 8X. Under the N.A.A.C.C. table of standards, this 8X material was rated at a breaking strength of four ounces. Imagine the problem of trying to handle a good-size fish on that kind of material. Today, nylon leader of the same diameter is rated at 7X and is four times as strong, far more uniform, and limp enough to allow a fly to float more freely and without drag.

Ordinary methods of handling fish did not work with fine silkworm gut. I was smashed time after time until I discovered what I was doing wrong. The trouble lay in the fact that an upright rod creates a lot of friction on a free-running line, and this friction uses up too much of the margin of safety of fine gut.

Strangely, only a few anglers in the history of fly-fishing seem to have discovered this fact and used it to advantage. One of the most famous of these—and perhaps the most successful salmon fishermen of all time—was A. H. E. Wood of Scotland, inventor of greased-line and low-water fishing for salmon. Wood invariably put his rod tip about one foot above the surface of the water and kept it there during a fight with a salmon. He caught thousands of salmon, many on 1X silkworm gut (N.A.A.C.C. test: one and one half pounds), using the low rod and no more pressure than that of the currents and the reel check. When queried about his low-rod technique, Wood said: "After all, there is little sense in continually pulling upward as though you were trying to lift the fish out of the river; and it only makes him more determined to get his head down and fight hard."

I feel the same way. I like to keep a big fish as calm and quiet as possible and lick him by nagging him to death a little at a time. On a low rod and loose line he becomes confused, and you can gently tow him out of danger by tugging lightly on the line with your thumb and forefinger.

Stiffness or softness of a rod has little bearing on the matter of fighting a trout on a delicate leader. If anything, the soft rod creates more friction and drag on the line than a stiff one does, because under full bend the soft rod assumes a more nearly complete circle, with the line bearing hard on every guide. The stiff rod bends only a little, usually near the top, creating severe line friction on only one or two guides.

Lowering the rod when you are using an ultrafine tippet

gives you a chance to adjust the drag with mathematical precision because you are playing your fish directly from the reel, which usually has tension adjustments. On the reel itself you need no more than one ounce of drag to prevent the line from overrunning. And remember that this drag may build up to two and one half or three ounces as the line runs out and comes closer to the core of the reel. Always adjust your reel with a full drum, not an empty one.

Another real danger to your fine tippet occurs when a strong fish makes a long run downriver and then suddenly turns and heads back up. This maneuver throws a wide loop in the line against which the current pushes with tremendous force. The lowered rod reduces this hazard a great deal, since the line will peel more freely from the reel.

One of the worst dangers is the jumping fish. Any hooked gamefish soon discovers what is bothering him, and he will often make a jump and try to fall on the leader or smash it with his tail. Here, again, the lowered rod allows the line to yield directly from the reel.

It is virtually impossible for a fish to throw a hook on a slack line. Hooks sometimes get a light hold on a mere thread of tissue and then tear out when the fisherman doesn't yield with the rod. I have landed many good fish that were barely hooked.

The most spectacular performance I ever saw involving a trout hooked on *Caenis* tackle happened in July 1968. Denis Nawrocki, George Green, John Faller, and I had gone to a small limestone stream near Carlisle, Pennsylvania, for a morning of *Caenis* fishing. We began fishing near the upstream end of a very long meadow. Denis was fishing a short distance below me, and suddenly I heard him give a whoop. I turned and was astonished to see a powerful trout plowing a furrow downstream and Denis with rod pointing downstream running madly over the rough terrain after the fish. Then both of them disappeared around a bend in the stream.

I took out after them as fast as my rickety joints would allow, all the while shouting a warning to Denis about the dangers below the bend. Denis was not familiar with this water. Below that bend was a sunken footbridge that caught and held debris that was washed downstream. If the trout got to the footbridge, all would be lost.

The trout stopped a few yards short of the bridge, and John Faller and I got out on it and flogged the water with our nets, trying to keep the fish upstream. The flogging succeeded for a while, but then the fish turned and blasted his way through the debris under our feet. I turned and was relieved to see Denis's white line deep in the water and running downstream.

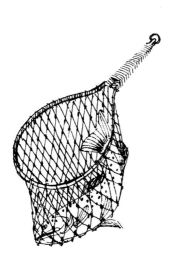

We pondered the situation for a few moments. Then, when the fish had stopped, I suggested to Denis that he separate his line from the reel while I fished the line out of the water below the bridge with a long pole.

It worked. Denis came below the bridge and refastened his line to the reel. Shortly thereafter we were able to net the fish many yards below the bridge.

Thus ended the prettiest race I ever saw between man and trout. Denis and that trout—a deep-girthed small-headed beautifully colored brown—must have run a quarter of a mile downstream.

So much for handling fish on *Caenis* tackle. Now let's look at the flies themselves.

The smallest practical imitation that I have used successfully is a No. 24. I have tried 28s, but I had such poor results in hooking and holding fish that I no longer use them.

I also had very poor results with the 24s until I began doctoring the hooks a little. The only 24s that I have been able to get have turned-down eyes, which close the bite of the hooks considerably. With a tiny jeweler's pliers I take hold of the neck of the hook just behind the eye and bend the eye upward a trifle, thus opening the bite. Next, with the hook in the vise, I push the shank laterally to either side to get the point out of alignment with the shank, thus opening the bite some more. I break a few hooks this way, but the results are really worthwhile. Finally, I sharpen the hook point by honing it gently with a hard Arkansas engraver's pencil.

Now we are ready to construct our imitation. The Leonards have reported six species of *Caenis*. The British claim four, but for a hundred years they have treated all four species as one. For practical purposes we can do the same.

The *Caenis* mayfly exists in four variations: male and female dun, and male and female spinner. By far the most important imitation is that of the female spinner, which falls to the water in vast numbers. The male spinner usually falls on land and is comparatively unimportant.

The female spinner has clear glassy wings; rear segments of the body are a translucent grayish white; the thorax is black and humped. The freshly emerged duns riding the currents are well taken by the trout, but here we can treat both sexes as one since they are so similar in appearance, their outstanding feature being the smoky blue wings. My favorite pattern for the dun is a simple and ancient fly, the Blue Upright:

> *Hook:* No. 24.
> *Tails:* three very short blue dun fibers, slanting downward to raise the hook as much as possible.
> *Body:* stripped bicolor peacock quill.
> *Hackle:* one or two tiny blue dun hackles no more than 1/8 inch long in the fiber to make a total hackle spread of 1/4 inch. Three or four turns are sufficient.

Natural blue dun hackle is preferable, of course. I am still eking out a few flies from an ancient blue dun neck. How I wish I had another one that was just like it.

As an alternate pattern, if you have only large blue dun hackles, you can bunch some fibers together and make blue wings in the same way that lemon wood-duck fibers are used. One or two turns of a tiny badger or cream hackle can be added to float the fly.

The following is one of Frederic Halford's fine patterns. It imitates very well the white curse, which is really the female spinner of the species:

Hook: No. 24.
Hackle: a tiny badger hackle, over three turns of black ostrich herl worked at the shoulder.
Body: black tying silk with flat silver tag.

No tails are mentioned by Halford, but I would add three short blue dun fibers, as for the previous pattern.

The following pattern is a great favorite with many local fishermen, primarily to imitate the female spinner:

Hook: No. 24.
Tails: three fibers of palest blue dun.
Body: grayish white fur, sparsely applied.
Thorax: a few turns of bronze peacock herl.
Hackle: badger or palest cream or blue dun.

Here is one of G. E. M. Skues's favorite patterns:

Hook: No. 22 or 24.
Wings: palest starling.
Body: white silk.
Hackle: a tiny white cock's hackle.

My favorite pattern for the female spinner is as follows:

Hook: No. 24.
Tails: three fibers of palest blue dun or palest cream hackle.

Body: two layers of clear white horsehair; start at the center of the shank, wind to the bend, then back to center again.

Thorax: black fur or black Angus wool (wonderful stuff that I collected from a barbed-wire fence).

Hackle: two or three turns of a tiny blue dun or palest cream hackle.

On all spinner patterns, keep the hackle thin. If the hackle turns out so thick that it obscures the body, cut away some fibers at top and bottom.

No matter what pattern you use, do not lose confidence in it if it is not immediately taken. *Caenis* fishing requires a lot of precision casting, and even then your fly is just one item among the many naturals that will be floating by the trout. So don't give up. The important thing is to get the trout to see your fly.

Finally, a few words about the strike—a fearful word in the language of the fly-fisherman if he knows all that it implies. A. H. E. Wood used a very unusual and successful method of setting the hook. He put the rod low and to the side of the fish and let the current pull the hook into the corner of the trout's mouth—and he took a lot of time to do it. The corner hold is the best of all, but we do not have enough current in our meadow streams to use the Wood method.

The best method I know of is to move the rod low and to the rear of the trout until the line is taut. That's all. The little hook will be drawn back to the corner of the fish's mouth, where it will embed itself firmly in the tough tissue in that area. The important point is to be deliberate. Your trout won't really come into contact with that little hook until he drops back and squeezes the water out of his mouth through his gills.

Caenis fishing is not a story of behemoth trout and two-handed adventure. It is an extremely sophisticated sport involving delicate tackle and the precise handling thereof. It can be very frustrating, but to me it will be forever the most fascinating kind of fishing.

II

The foregoing section, published originally as a magazine piece, is repeated here not only because it is still a timely subject but also because of its historical value as the first publication in America dealing with this important phase of fly-fishing. To many people it is a mystery that *Caenis* fishing remained unsung and unstoried for such a long time. It is easily explained.

Prior to 1957 the legal trout-fishing season in Pennsylvania ended on July 31 of each year. I am sure that similar short legal seasons prevailed in many other states. Since the emergence date of *Caenis* as a fishing hatch is somewhere in the last two weeks of July, only the few people who lived nearby could experience and enjoy this hatch near the end of the season.

For many years in my lifetime and that of my contemporaries there was a great and aching void suffered by all dedicated trout fishermen from the end of July until the hunting season. It was for this reason that many of us turned to bass and Atlantic salmon fishing in late summer and early fall. For me, these were second choices. It was a situation that was particularly frustrating to me because I knew what fine fly-fishing could be had on Pennsylvania trout streams in late summer and early fall. This is a long pleasant weather period in Pennsylvania, especially in the southern half of the state, and during this period there are new enduring hatches of small and large mayflies as well as the enormously important terrestrial fishing now familiar to everyone. New generations of fly-fishermen are fortunate to be able to enjoy these new opportunities because of the extension of the legal season, at first to September 1 and, more recently, to October 31.

There was another handicap that prevented exploitation of small-fly and late-season fishing. It was the matter of constructing artificials small enough to match the many tiny insects that prevailed. Older generations, including mine, were brought up on a philosophy that dictated the use of artificials no smaller than size 16. As a matter of fact, many professional tiers refused to tie anything smaller. In addition, there were no hooks smaller than size 20 available. The smallest that I could find, after much searching and inquiry, were size 20 short shank. These were not satisfactory. The availability in recent years of hooks smaller than size 20 has changed the entire picture, and now it is unusual to meet a fly-fisherman who cannot tie and use these tiny flies successfully.

The proper artificial for *Caenis* fishing is no longer a problem but there are certain aspects, procedural in nature, that I have not discussed or about which I have not written. They involve the behaviorism and particularly the rise patterns of the trout during the hatch. This is, of course, a continuing expression of the theme of this book.

I have stated often that the *Caenis* hatch is one of amazing regularity. The trout, too, acquire a peculiar regularity connected with the hatch. After the hatch has been in progress for a few weeks, the trout begin to anticipate it. Many times, upon arrival at the stream early in the morning, before the duns and spinners begin to show, the water appears to be lifeless, without activity of any kind; then, as the mist lifts and the atmosphere brightens, I can see with binoculars a trout here and there lifting to the surface and there they remain poised and waiting, with that alert look about them, plainly indicating by their attitudes that they know what is coming.

At this stage they are easily spooked, darting away to cover if you approach too closely and are seen. Once the hatch begins, there is a remarkable change of character. The feeding on *Caenis* is usually very rapid, and so intent are the fish on getting their shares that they bcome oblivious to the near presence of the fisherman. This is a lucky circumstance because it means that the fisherman can get close, use a short line, and make the rapid, accurate casts needed in this fishing. The overriding consideration at all times is the need for extreme accuracy. In a

heavy hatch such as you may encounter with *Caenis*, there are so many naturals from which to choose that it is impossible to get the trout's attention with your tiny artificial, lost among a deluge of tiny naturals. You have a chance only if you pass your artificial rapidly and accurately over his nose, in his line of drift; but this must be done as for any good cast—lightly and without a vestige of drag. The pickup is the critical point in this rapid casting. Most of the time you cannot see your fly being taken and a violent pickup results in a smashed leader, a precious lost fly and, worst of all, loss of valuable time in retying. For a brief instant the pickup must be started slowly, then accelerated to begin your next cast. It is a highly demanding, finely timed, highly disciplined kind of casting. A recipe for this kind of casting would read as follows: two rapid flicks of the fly in the air to remove moisture; a short accurate pass over the trout; brief, slow pickup; two rapid flicks in the air; and then repeat.

Now let us examine further some of the rise patterns during the *Caenis* hatch. Perhaps the most difficult of all for the fisherman is the habit of many trout to shift from side to side while feeding on dun or spinner. It is obvious that you cannot pitch to the last riseform if he is going to shift to his right side for his next insect. Your fly would pass too far to the left and would be ignored. The same result would occur in the reverse situation. The real difficulty here lies in the fact that the shift is very often unbalanced; that is, instead of taking one on the right, then one on the left, he may take two on the right and one on the left, thus wasting your cast on the left where you anticipated his next move. You can abandon such a fish and try for another, but if he is a real trophy, you will stay with him until you catch him, making the anticipated shift in the direction of your fly.

I wish to emphasize as strongly as possible that it is important to see your fish or at least try to see him. With all the shifting about that they do, it is not easy to determine a rise pattern for a particular fish and you may be led into thinking that a number of scattered rises are being made by a number of individuals instead of by only one fish. It is not easy to tell you how to go about seeing your fish but perhaps if we listen again to Major Hills, in his *A Summer on the Test*, we may learn how it is done. He prescribed it better than anyone else that I know, as follows:

> You must cultivate an eye for water and an eye for trout. The gift is not easily attained: in all cases it requires practice; and some never acquire it. But it can be learned by nine people out of ten. It is learned by what seems easy but is hard: looking at the water. Looking at it not lightly or casually but examining it intently, boring into it, determining to penetrate its hidden recesses.
>
> You must make up your mind that if there are trout in the river you will see them.
>
> Trout are dim, uncertain and nearly invisible. You learn after a time where to look and what to look for. You must not expect to see a whole trout, outlined as though lying on a fishmonger's slab: Any fool can see that: but what you have to train yourself to pick out is a flicker, a movement, a darkness, a luminosity, which if you stare at it hard enough will resolve itself into a shadowy form. It may be weed, or a reflection, or a shaft of light through the wavering water; but on the other hand it may be a trout: whenever therefore you pitch upon anything unexpected or surprising which by remote chance may be a fish, never leave it until you have solved its riddle. You will waste time on stones or gravel or sticks or such-like, but it is remarkable how you improve and nothing improves you so quickly as being with someone who is good at the game.

There are two additional ways of spotting trout in the water that I shall add to Major Hills's prescription. One of them is to move about, back and forth until you see a clear spot on the surface where the light is polarized, that is, where it moves in one direction, penetrating the water and not reflected back to you. There is always such a spot. The second way is feasible where there is a light-colored stream bottom and the water is

"You must cultivate an eye for water and an eye for trout. . . . You must make up your mind that if there are trout in the river, you will see them."

clear. In such places trout take on the same coloration as the stream bottom and are virtually invisible. Look for an unexplained shadow on the bottom of the stream because trout are opaque and will cast a shadow no matter how well camouflaged they may be. That is the way I used to spot them in the shallow headwaters of Big Spring at Newville, Pennsylvania.

Of course, if you are fishing very late to a fall of spinners when there is no way to see your fish in the darkness, there is still a positive way of locating your fish and casting very accurately to him—in fact, as accurately as in the daytime. It is a method that I worked out in connection with my fishing to the spinner fall of *Ephoron leukon* on the Yellow Breeches. There is usually enough light going, even in the pitch darkness, to create a tiny luminous flash when the trout rises and breaks the surface. Lengthen or shorten your casts and retrieve your fly sharply each time so as to scratch the water and create a luminous glow of your own. By adjusting your flash to that of the trout, you can eventually make normal floats and gentle pickups in the same line of drift in which he is feeding. You cannot, of course, detect any shifting by the trout in the darkness but I am positive that they do not shift during the *leukon* fall of spinners. I have caught many trout in the darkness with this method.

Trout are highly individualistic in the kinds of rise patterns that they make. Some make a very broad shift, moving across stream in a progressive shift during which they pick off an insect every few inches that they move across stream. A fish may take half a dozen in this way, then move across the line of drift to the right, picking off successive insects in the same manner. It is far easier to anticipate his moves in the progressive shift than in the unbalanced shift mentioned above. There is an interesting variation to the progressive shift that I shall describe as a diagonal shift. In this one he moves across and upstream as well. The only real problem here is that you must lengthen the cast with each move because on each take he will be moving further away from you. Sometimes this movement is an upstream progression—no diagonal involvement. The casting problem is the same. In each instance, whether diagonal or upstream, when he has reached the limit of his chosen range he will make an uninterrupted return to his original starting point and repeat the same pattern over and over again.

There is a rise pattern that is the reverse of the diagonal and upstream progressions. In this one the trout continually drops downstream, tail first, picking off insects as he goes; then, when he reaches the chosen limit of his range, he makes an

uninterrupted move upstream to his original starting point and does the same thing over and over again. The important thing to remember is that you must keep moving downstream in order to stay below your trout or else you will find yourself pulling upstream on the strike, bouncing that little hook over the bony front of his jaws instead of catching it in the tough tissue of the corner where you want it.

Finally, there is that peculiar rise pattern made by some trout, often big ones, when the duns and spinners are extremely thick on the water. The trout takes up a fixed position, then rises very rapidly, actually gobbling like a duck as Frank Sawyer describes it. The rises may be as rapid as one every second. He lifts and falls on the clusters of insects like a man making rapid push-ups. With each fall there is a peculiar sound that suggests that he is slapping the water with the roof of his mouth. This slapstrike can be accurately simulated by slapping the forefinger of one hand sharply into the palm of the other hand. Once you have heard it, you will never forget it. When I showed this rise pattern to the late Joe Brooks some years ago, he was fascinated and would stop fishing to listen and watch it. I like to catch a big fish doing this because you need only use a little careful timing to run the fly right into his open mouth!

I have said that rapid casts and short floats are the general rule in *Caenis* fishing. There are, however, a few exceptions. Sometimes you may find in well-stocked waters a number of trout occupying a choice line of drift, all lined up, in tandem, one behind the other like beggars in a lineup waiting for a handout.

This is the time to make a long float, and nothing is better than the puddle cast for this purpose, dropping the fly accurately with many loose coils at the head of the lineup and riding it down through the whole gang without fear or favor. You never know which one will take your fly and most of the time you cannot even see which has taken it. If you see a rise near the suspected position of your tiny fly, lift gently so as to prevent a smash, and if there is no fish attached, pick up and start the fly through again. In this way I have scored heavily, many times hooking, losing, and landing as many as thirty fish in a single morning.

Elsewhere I have described in great detail the habit of drifting with the insect and making a reverse strike. This happens very often during the *Caenis* hatch. If you should see a fish doing this repeatedly, then it is time to make the long float again; otherwise you will have no chance to take the fish if your fly drags before he can catch up with it and take it. Another situation that demands a long float occurs where a good big trout occupies a position where he can be reached only with a long downstream cast. I suggest that you ignore the little trout in this situation; only the big ones are worth the risk involved in this kind of a cast. Usually you get only one chance with this cast and a tiny fly. If he takes, you must pull the little hook upstream against the bony front of his mouth. You will be lucky to hook him. If he does not take, the fly will drag heavily and you will have no more chances, but it is worth a try.

Until now I have refrained from discussing tackle for *Caenis* fishing, since it is a specialized matter. I have had many opportunities to observe the kind of tackle used by fishermen who come in great numbers to visit and fish my limestone waters during the *Caenis* season. Most of it is satisfactory but some of it is woefully unsuitable. My long association with the *Caenis* hatch, plus the fact that so much of my fishing during the year involves the use of small flies, made me very much aware that certain refinements in tackle would be desirable and helpful. I was particularly concerned about the kind of rod that should be used for this fishing.

I have always been partial to the longer rods—eight feet or more. In *Caenis* and other small-fly fishing, the leader gets longer because of the addition of long, fine tippets, without which the little fly won't behave properly—and you cannot puddle a cast very well with short leaders. Thus, a normal nine-and-a-half- or ten-foot leader may become a thirteen- or four-

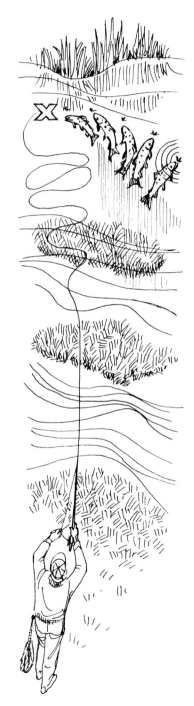

teen-foot leader and nothing—I repeat, nothing—will handle a long leader as efficiently as a long rod will. But length is no virtue if it means a cumbersome, slow-moving, insensitive rod.

I have described the nature of the casting during the *Caenis* hatch: fast, delicate, accurate. Eventually, I set about to design and make a rod to suit these requirements. The completed rod that I now use is eight and a half feet long and weighs only three and a half ounces in spite of the fact that it is a three-piece rod carrying the weight of two sets of ferrules and an aluminum bank spear in the butt so that I can keep the rod upright, out of harm's way, when it is not in use. I am sure that I could reduce the weight considerably more by eliminating one set of ferrules and the bank spear, but I prefer the rod as it is. The rod is designed so that only the tip works in delivering short rapid casts of twenty-five or thirty feet. When the casts are lengthened the workload is thrown back on the second joint, which was designed to bend and relieve the tip section. The butt joint is fairly stiff, thus confining the action to the upper two-thirds to ensure less weave and greater accuracy. I have described the design principles in an earlier chapter. It is a thoroughly delightful rod to use, light in the hand, fast moving, sensitive, and accurate.

In appraising and evaluating the *Caenis* hatch, I have often used superlatives that may have seemed excessive to many. I do not retract any of them. I still regard this hatch as the finest of all mayfly hatches. I have good reasons for saying so. This hatch provides one of the most fascinating and exotic experiences in fly-fishing—namely, the frequent hooking and oftentimes the landing of big trout on minimal tackle. Every time this happens to me it seems like a new and richer experience. I have caught my good share of eighteen- to twenty-inchers on 7X tippets and size 24 flies and hooked larger ones that I did not land, but I am not so blasé about my sport that I do not experience a quickening of the heartbeat and a catch in my breath when I see a big buster of a trout rocking gently up and down, sipping those ridiculously small flies—and I must confront such fish with my puny tackle. I would dispute vehemently Ernest Hemingway's assertion that only bullfighters live life to the hilt. Fly-fishermen, too!

A strange thing happens to a fisherman who hooks a really big fish on fine tackle. It is not an easy thing to explain and only someone who has had the experience will fully understand what I say. I have an acquaintance who insists that it is akin to a sexual experience but I will deny that out of hand. Perhaps I can best explain this "strange thing" by telling a story about a friend of mine with whom I went fishing one day during the *Caenis* season. We were widely separated at riverside but I heard his faint shout and turned to see him engaged with a fish.

His attitude and the arched rod convinced me that he was into something big. I speared my rod in the bank, grabbed my big long-handled landing net, and ran to offer whatever assistance I could. It was indeed a big trout. I could see him very clearly, every detail—the large spots, the thick body, and the beautiful crimson and gold colors of a streambred brown trout. I remained close to my companion and together, for one solid hour, we followed that trout everywhere he went. He was using the standard tackle of 7X leader and 24 fly and he was using it skillfully. Four times during that hour, the trout streaked under a low footbridge, forcing my companion to pass his rod underneath and recover it from the other side.

Finally, the big trout quit his wild surges and dove into a weed bed on the other bank. I could see clearly the hole he made entering the weed bed and his broad tail sticking out of the hole. I realized quickly that it was a golden opportunity to give my companion an unforgettable day by climaxing the adventure with the capture of that fish. He would not have killed it I am sure but the photographs that he liked to take would have been precious to him. I was standing very close to my companion and I begged him for permission to go in and land that fish with my big long-handled net. I have done it many

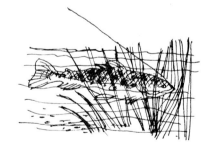

times under the same circumstances and was sure that I could do it this time. He did not answer me. Again I repeated my request, this time with more urgency and again he refused to answer me. I did not pursue the matter any further but I looked closely at my companion and could see that familiar trancelike attitude, head high, mouth slightly agape, his eyes wide and staring. It was plain that he was oblivious to everything in his surroundings except himself, that big fish, and the fragile connection between them. He was in the grip of a profound abstraction of mind and spirit. Shortly thereafter the big trout came out of the hole, drove hard upstream, shaking his head violently, and broke the frail tippet.

In the aftermath of this event, when we could talk calmly about the incident, I asked him why he would not give me permission to go in and net the fish. He was astonished when I told him what had happened and he confessed that he never heard my repeated request!

I am continually amazed by the sight of large trout that take these tiny insects and I have not yet determined the limit in size of the trout that will eat them. I knew of one six-pounder that would eat them but that fish was eventually caught and killed on something less sublime than a dainty *Caenis* artificial. To be sure, trout of six pounds or more do not eat in that way very often, but I am convinced that it does happen. I have a very vivid recollection of an incident that happened a few years ago when I was fishing the *Caenis* on one of my favorite limestoners. I was walking the bank slowly and softly, scanning the water carefully for some sign of feeding activity when I spotted, low in the water, what was certainly the form of a big fish. His size was really impressive but I was not sure that it was a trout and because of my uncertainty a dreadful thought occurred to me. O Lord, I said to myself, "When did the carp get into this fine trout stream?" I was occupied with this dark thought briefly when to my amazement he rose to the surface and appeared to take something. There was a short pause, then he did the same thing a second time. It was no carp! I watched for a considerable length of time thereafter but that fish never rose again. I was duty bound, of course, to try for that fish, but my few casts were entirely ignored, as I expected, so I went on my way to seek a more reasonable kind of fishing. That fish might have been taken on a big wet fly and coarse tippet but I did not want it in that manner.

If I had been able to hook such a fish as I saw that day on my small tackle, it would have been nothing but an idle gesture on my part. In the weed-choked waters that I fish you need not only skill but also a great deal of luck with big fish on fine tackle. In open water with no obstructions or possible entanglements, I am sure that a skillful fisherman could land a ten-pounder on today's 6X and a sound 24 hook—if you could get that kind of fish to take that size of fly.

The large size of the trout often encountered in *Caenis* fishing is not the only reason for my lavish praise. The *Caenis* hatch is unquestionably the most widespread across the land. It flourishes on many streams in the East, in freestone as well as limestone rivers. It is a major hatch in midwestern trout rivers. It is equally important in many rivers of the Far West. The same fly with the same characteristics thrives in Europe. The British have been familiar with it for a long time but won't exploit it because they are still laboring under the notion that a hook smaller than size 16 or 17 is of no practical use. What a pity!

One of the special blessings connected with *Caenis* is the fact that it is a daytime hatch unlike many of the highly touted hatches of other mayflies. And it is eagerly taken by the trout in all its phases—nymph, dun, and spinner—unlike many other mayflies.

This hatch is extremely reliable in its annual appearance, varying little in its emergence dates.

Finally, it is the most enduring of all hatches, at least on eastern waters, providing in many areas a daily unfailing rise of trout for four or more months, beginning in July and ending in November.

No other mayfly can measure up to all these valuable attributes.

Chapter Seven

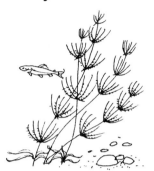

Big Fly: Big Trout

I GLANCED QUICKLY AT THE FRAME COUNTER ON MY CAMERA AND WAS astonished to find that I had almost finished my third roll of film for the afternoon. And it was color film, not the comparatively inexpensive black and white.

Still the wild orgy continued as one grasshopper after another thrashed the water desperately in a futile effort to escape the demanding current and the uncompromising jaws of a big brown trout that was collecting his dinner.

One exposure at a time is expensive enough, but a friend of

mine, Bob McCormick, special assistant to the governor on conservation and natural resources and one of the last of the big spenders, was shooting in bursts of three on each rise. Someone in the appreciative gallery behind us suggested that it didn't really sound like a camera but more like a cash register.

This was grasshopper time on the Letort, a gentle little river near Carlisle, Pennsylvania, where trout grow big. Once, long ago, I raised and hooked one of those big browns, and the performance of that monster was so fantastic that I never dared tell the whole truth about the encounter. Once or twice when I tried to tell it, I was greeted with stony silence and a few indulgent smiles that indicated my exaggerations were pardonable as long as I was just talking for effect.

But things have changed. During the years, enough trout have been seen and caught in these waters by a host of new and enterprising fishermen that my legendary trout now seems a very credible creature indeed. Don Martin's fifteen-and-a-half-pounder caught at Big Spring Creek, Newville, Pennsylvania, in June 1945 was the first of the giant brown trout taken in these native brook trout waters.

During the intervening years, there have been many four- and five-pounders taken and, more recently, some in the eight- to ten-pound class.

Amazingly, many of these big trout have been caught on dry flies. And this fly-fishing is being done on the small, fertile, limestone streams of central Pennsylvania, which in many places can be spanned by a first-class jumper.

To get back to my big trout, it was on a Saturday afternoon in late season almost twenty years ago that Charlie Fox and I discovered him, and we first heard rather than saw him. There were violent splashing sounds coming from a section of the Letort not immediately visible to us. We hurried toward the commotion and finally saw something that neither of us will ever forget. We witnessed the most fantastic and incredible kind of a surface strike imaginable. It was an enormous brown trout, larger than either of us had ever seen. The idea of a trout that size in such a small stream was unbelievable.

His rises to the drifting and scratching grasshoppers were so spectacular and so violent that the banks of the stream were drenched with spray ten feet beyond the edge of the water. I have watched twenty-pound Atlantic salmon rise to a dry fly, but it was never so impressive as this sight. We were a little awestricken and just stood watching this fantastic exhibition. Eventually, we quietly backed off to discuss the situation.

I was desperately eager to try for that fish. Charlie understood and generously told me to go ahead while he sought a concealed vantage point from which he could watch the trout's movements and help direct my casts. This is the kind of teamwork we have been successful with for many years.

Remembrance of that occasion after so many years is now dreamlike, but I can vividly recall the apprehensive moments as I crawled on hands and knees to get into position, freezing every time Charlie called to warn me that the trout was looking my way. I also recall that this fish, when chasing a flailing grasshopper close to my position, threw water up onto my fly box while I was trying to extract a suitable imitation. That didn't help my composure one bit.

I made many futile casts on that long Saturday afternoon, but not one of my poor, improvised imitations was convincing enough. After all, what good is a No. 14 Hendrickson when something as big and definitive as the grasshopper is required?

We left the Letort that evening with a deep sense of frustration and bafflement. One thing was certain: I didn't have a decent imitation of a grasshopper in my fly box. So I spent a few hours with no great conviction tying a few fancied imitations of the grasshopper.

I rooted among my possessions hoping to find something more satisfactory. I turned up only one likely prospect, a peculiar-looking thing, fashioned from a hollow quill, with horns at the head, short hackle-quill legs at the sides, and a pale green, painted quill body. It was a gift, ignored for a time, but now I looked at it with renewed interest and put it into my fly box.

The one dread that gnawed at me all evening was the possibility that I might not have another chance at that same fish.

I didn't sleep well that night. Over and over again I reviewed events and wondered how I might have avoided failure.

I was awake early the next morning, prepared for action long before Charlie arrived to join me. Both of us expressed the same anxiety during that seemingly long ride to the Letort. We dared to hope that the trout would be in the same place, feeding just as he had been doing the day before.

Imagine our elation when we found him feeding again, and even more violently than on the previous afternoon. I got into position as quickly as possible and, after some hesitation, chose that quill-bodied imitation I just described. After the second or third cast (I was never sure which one), the surface exploded, and my imitation disappeared in a three-foot arc of flying spray. Momentarily a great calm came over me, and I lifted the rod gently until line and leader were taut. Then I flexed the rod tip hard to drive the hook home.

Charlie rushed to join me, and now both of us stood there tense, expectant, waiting to see which way the fish would go. Nothing happened. He simply lay there—quiet and solid. It was as if I had hooked a submerged stump.

Finally, after what seemed a long time, he turned and swam leisurely downstream to a large weed bed; then he sank to the bottom and burrowed among the weeds into the mud on the downstream side.

This is a trick that a hooked trout often uses in the weedy Letort, and I knew exactly what to do. Moving below him, I put the rod tip low, almost touching the water, and hauled back with all the pressure I dared. Ordinarily this method is successful, causing a trout to back out of the weeds when he no longer can maintain a position against the downstream pressure. But not this trout—not immediately anyway.

Strike!

Struck!

Stricken!

It got very tiresome, holding the rod that way, and I had to slack off now and then to rest a little. At last there seemed to be a slight stirring in the weed bed, a faint yielding that was encouraging. Gradually the pressure diminished until finally the trout turned and moved leisurely downstream to burrow into another weed bed.

So it went for two long weary hours, from weed bed to weed bed, the strangest, dreariest, most discouraging experience I had ever had with a trout. I wish I could tell an exciting story of dashing runs and great flashing leaps accompanied by a screaming reel. It just didn't happen that way. In fact, it got so boring and muscle fatiguing that I sat or knelt most of the time, holding the rod with two hands, sometimes propping my elbows on my knees for additional support.

After two hours of this dogged fight, I called Charlie's attention to the accumulation of weeds burdening my line and asked him if he could do something about it. Charlie carefully eased himself into the water, held the line, and cautiously removed the dangerous collection of weeds.

Charlie stood still a moment, staring intently into the clear waters of the Letort. Then he made a short, sharp exclamation and turned toward me, wide-eyed, with his hands cupped and spread apart an astonishing distance to indicate the barrellike proportions of the monster that I had hooked.

The next and final half hour brought a distinct change in tactics. The trout abandoned the weed beds, rose higher toward the surface, and began to turn in small circles. Almost immediately I felt an unpleasant jarring sensation in my rod hand. I felt it two or three times before I discovered what was happening.

I looked closely at the water, and there I saw the awful length of him near the surface making those tight circles and slapping the leader with that massive tail at every turn. Now I understood the jarring sensation and quickly reeled in line, stretching arm and rod out as far as possible in a horizontal plane to place the rod point almost over his back.

This trick kept the leader turning perpendicular to his head, preventing any further leader slapping. After a few futile attempts, he gave up the slapping and went to the bottom again. It didn't help him though. He was tiring fast now and couldn't hold his position against the constant perpendicular lift, maintained by two very tired arms. I was determined to see an end to this weird contest.

Finally, he stayed at the surface and wallowed, his dorsal fin and tail breaking the surface. Now I had a clear look at him, not distorted by refraction. He was longer than a yardstick, deep, potbellied, and square, and he had the red orange fins and tail typical of stream-fed trout.

These things I saw as I towed him gently toward a little bay. That trout was thoroughly licked. I hadn't made a mistake. He lay there absolutely helpless, unable to move a fin. All that remained was the business of landing him.

And now for the first time, the stark realization of the problem that confronted us struck me: how to land such a fish.

An Atlantic salmon of the same size would have been easy to land without net or gaff because a salmon has stiff, bony spines at the edges of his tail that enable the fisherman to grab and hand-tail his fish. But a trout's tail has no rigid, bony spines. If you try to take him by the tail, it collapses and squirts through your hand, a disappointing experience.

We had no gaff, no net of adequate size, and no shallows where he could be scooped or dragged. Helpless, and completely fascinated by the thing in front of us, we stood and stared while I held him in the little bay.

Then suddenly the leader snapped, and we watched in hypnotic silence as the great trout slowly sank out of sight.

Almost twenty years have passed since that eventful day, and Charlie and I have discussed and relived that experience many times. He insists that I will never again hook such a trout. Perhaps he is right. One thing is sure: Whether I again hook such a trout or not, I will continue to carry the same salmon-size net I have carried ever since that experience.

It seems anomalous that I had my most remarkable trout-fishing experience in the early days when I knew little or nothing about fishing in grasshopper season, but actually this incident, followed by a chain of related events, occurred at an opportune time. Together they provided stimulus for a handful of eager young men who brought about a real revolution in fly-fishing on the banks of the beautiful Letort and Big Spring Creek.

Grasshopper fishing is only another phase of this upheaval. There were additional facets: Japanese beetles, red and black ants, and crickets, as well as the vast variety of tiny, land-born insects collectively called jassids. All of them flourish in the long, dry summer period when fly-fishing was traditionally abandoned and ignored.

Older outdoor writers used to repeat religiously that fly-fishing was not worthwhile after the big mayfly hatches were over. Some writers are still saying it. Some of them say also that really big trout cannot be taken regularly on dry flies. At one time I was willing to accept this dictum. But no more.

Late-season fishing with terrestrial-insect imitations is changing the whole trout-fishing picture. These terrestrial imitations are certainly attractive to big trout. But the underlying reason for increased catches of big trout on dry flies is that big trout migrate late in the season out of deep, inaccessible holes into shallows where they can be tempted with dry flies.

Dry-fly fishing is really a shallow-water affair. It is never so good in deep rivers or streams. This migration of big trout is undoubtedly preliminary to the spawning period in late fall and winter and would not have been apparent before, when legal trout-fishing seasons were much shorter. Now these big fish are a late-season bonus for the dry-fly man.

The best of this fishing is yet to come. And it has come now that many legal seasons are extended into September and October, which are peak periods for the terrestrials and the renewal of some mayfly hatches.

On our waters in central Pennsylvania, the flights of winged ants and the hatches of *Baetis* mayflies in September and October are tremendous. They must be seen to be believed. Many times in October I have seen the surface of the Letort literally carpeted with *Baetis* and ants, and trout rising madly to both.

Traditional treatment by many older angling writers included only the water-bred insects—mostly mayflies and caddis flies. Inquiries began and ended at waterside. Rarely did old-timers look farther.

A Letort fisherman is a different breed. Half the time you may find him wandering about the meadows, entirely ignoring the water, kicking here and there in tall grass, stooping now and then to pluck and examine something, looking generally like anybody but a fisherman.

He may be a lover of roses, but his preoccupation with a wild rosebush on the bank has nothing to do with roses. You may find him tugging at a grapevine suspended from an ancient walnut tree, but he probably has little interest in grapes or walnuts.

Actually, in spite of appearances, he is a very sensible fellow tending to his fishing. His apparently aimless meandering amounts to very careful inspection of the primary source of his fishing—the abundant insect life born and bred in the rich meadows of the limestone country.

Truly he fishes as much in his meadows as he does in his waters. That is to say, the limestone fisherman has created an entirely new concept in stream management. The books will have to be rewritten. They will have to contain whole chapters on the management of these meadows that provide insect life for a superior kind of fishing.

Let us consider now some specifics about imitation grasshoppers. Exciting and continued experiences with big trout sent many of us scurrying about looking for a decent artificial. At that time the only commercial patterns available were the Palmer grasshopper, a cork-bodied floating imitation invented

in 1915 by M. Palmer of Pasadena, California; and the Michigan Hopper, which is a wool-bodied, turkey-winged pattern.

The Palmer grasshopper has never achieved any popularity in this area, but the Michigan fly caught on very well and is the basic pattern for many variations popular on the Letort and nearby streams. Some of the variations have clipped deerhair bodies and wings of hair or lacquered feathers tied flat over the backs of the grasshoppers. They are difficult to cast and difficult to float.

I too tried to tie a satisfactory imitation of the grasshopper but frankly never succeeded. My tale of discontent finally caught the attention of Bill Bennett, then a very active member of the Harrisburg fly-fishing fraternity and a first-rate flytier.

Bill became deeply interested in the problem and began to investigate all the angles involved. I recounted to Bill my strange experience with the giant trout and the quill-bodied grasshopper. He wanted to see the pattern. I had got the original from Charlie Craighead, a native Pennsylvanian born and raised on the Yellow Breeches Creek near Carlisle. I asked Charlie for another one, and eventually he tied one that I turned over to Bill. I will describe the outcome in Bill's own words, which were first published in 1950 in my book *A Modern Dry-Fly Code.*

My first attempt to improve Craighead's hopper resulted in partial failure, for my hopper, minus legs and plus oiled silk wings, floated on its side, whirled and buzzed disconcertingly while being cast, and was improved only to the extent that I had painted the quill body yellow instead of covering it with lacquered silk, thus eliminating the possibility of water-logging.

My next attempt was approached with a little more study. What we needed was a hopper that would float upright yet retain the general silhouette of the live hopper. The answer was the addition of two small quills on each side of the larger quill body—pontoons—which would serve a twofold purpose: first, to keep the hopper floating on even keel; and second, to simulate folded legs.

A hastily constructed model compared with a live hopper

quickly convinced me that my model closely resembled the general outlines of the real hopper afloat. That much behind me, I next turned to the construction of the body. To paint the quill seemed practical, but would it stand up on the underbody, which was to take quite a beating in long hours of casting? This problem, however, was solved quite accidentally; one night while rooting through my material cabinets I uncovered several dyed duck quill feathers in various colors. This was the answer, for I reasoned that if the quills were cut and prepared before dyeing, the dye would penetrate both inside and outside the quill, thus assuring a lasting translucent body color.

That is how Bill Bennett describes the development of the very finest grasshopper pattern I had ever seen. Its virtues far exceeded anything else being used then or now. It was absolutely colorfast because the color was locked inside the translucent, sealed quill. It floated upright no matter how badly cast and floated high and dry at the end of 5,000 casts as well as it floated on the first cast. It would float beautifully if it were cast into Niagara Falls. There is no better imitation hopper than Bill Bennett's Pontoon Hopper.

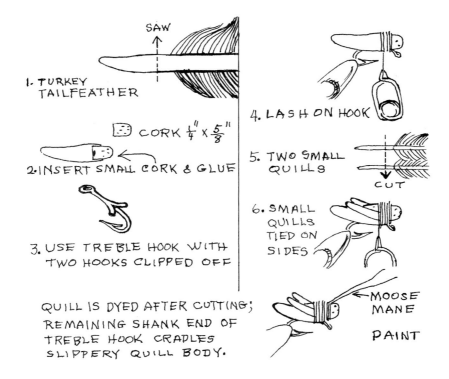

1. TURKEY TAILFEATHER

SAW

CORK ¼" × ⅝"

2. INSERT SMALL CORK & GLUE

3. USE TREBLE HOOK WITH TWO HOOKS CLIPPED OFF

QUILL IS DYED AFTER CUTTING; REMAINING SHANK END OF TREBLE HOOK CRADLES SLIPPERY QUILL BODY.

4. LASH ON HOOK

5. TWO SMALL QUILLS

CUT

6. SMALL QUILLS TIED ON SIDES

MOOSE MANE

PAINT

It has several additional virtues that could not be duplicated in a fur-and-feather concoction, Michigan style or otherwise. It is the most durable fly I have ever seen, and a single one could easily last for years. Next, because it floats so lightly, it is extremely sensitive. The slightest ripple or vagary in the current causes it to bob and weave astonishingly like a live grasshopper. The scratching and kicking of a live grasshopper on the water is an extremely difficult thing to simulate with an upstream cast and slack delivery.

By contrast, the big fur-and-feather imitation quickly becomes soggy and deadhearted.

With the Pontoon Hopper, there is an extra dividend, something that has nothing to do with trout fishing: This imitation is one of the deadliest bass bugs in the world. Make one, buy one, or steal one; take it to a bass pond or river shallow enough for bass bugging; and you will likely have a grand time.

With the increasing interest in late-season grasshopper fishing, new attempts have been made by other fishermen to create suitable patterns. I am indebted to John Alevras of Bloomfield, New Jersey, for a beautifully tied sample of a pattern whose origin I have not discovered. As far as I know, it has no name.

It involves the newer technique of tying a bundle of deerhair on a piece of stiff wire. This body is removed from the wire and tied to the neck of a No. 14 hook, short shank. Two thin clumps of deerhair are tied in at the sides to form legs.

This too is an unsinkable pattern. I have tried repeatedly to make it sink by slapping it hard on the surface, but it would not go down. It is a much easier fly to cast than the Pontoon Hopper, but it still lacks the sensitivity and the live appearance of the Pontoon Hopper. Nevertheless, it is a worthy pattern and has many more virtues than do older patterns of fur and hackle that become soggy, deadhearted floaters.

The development of this pattern was, I think, in response to complaints of many fishermen that the Pontoon Hopper is difficult to cast. It is, if it is tied too large. The Pontoon Hopper need not be longer than three-quarters of an inch, or an inch at most. The small hoppers are easier to cast and just as effective as the large ones.

How is such an imitation fished? In the beginning of this story, I mentioned my photographic activity with grasshoppers and feeding trout. In my career as a fly-fisherman I have wielded the camera and rod with equal fervor. The many hours spent in making camera studies of feeding fish have revealed far more fishing secrets than an equal number of hours spent with rod alone.

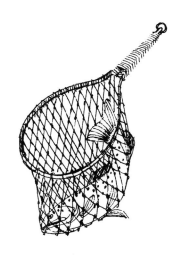

A photographic session with one feeding trout may result in seventy or eighty single exposures, which means that one big trout of let us say four or five pounds can eat seventy-five or eighty grasshoppers at a single feeding. Bass are equally voracious. With so much feeding activity, a trout is bound to reveal his preferences and his feeding habits. One of the most interesting of these revelations concerns the kind of grasshoppers he likes. It has nothing to do with scientific names. It has to do with the color.

He wants yellow grasshoppers.

It is amazing how decided this preference is. He will ignore a dozen of any other color to get a yellow one. The meadows contain an astonishing assortment of grasshoppers in different colors, more than I would have believed without a careful inspection of my own. They come in yellow, greenish yellow, green, brown, gray, black, and in different shades of these colors.

A trout gets to see all of them. At the peak of the season, hoppers are plentiful and as noisy as raindrops on a tin roof. They blunder about, flying aimlessly in any and every direction, seemingly without plan or purpose, and land on any kind of a surface, including the water.

Use nothing but yellow imitations, a butter yellow or maize color.

Our final and probably most important consideration involves the habits of a trout feeding on grasshoppers. And here again the camera studies reveal something to help us make a proper delivery of the artificial.

The grasshopper, being a landlubber, knows absolutely nothing about the water. He cannot possibly know of the existence of such a creature as a trout or that a trout might be waiting for him if he falls or jumps into the water. Nevertheless, he hates water. If he lands on it he becomes panic-stricken, scratching and furiously striving to get back to dry land as though he understood fully the disaster that awaits him. This panic apparently is communicated to trout. They become extremely excited and are stimulated far beyond their ordinary composure at a feeding station.

The same trout that under these circumstances makes frenzied slashes, lunges, and explosive rises for grasshoppers might be seen at another time sedately and gently rising and softly sipping tiny insects with unhurried good taste.

It takes only a few grasshoppers to put him in an awful state of excitement; then he begins to look for them, with shivery anticipation, far beyond his observation post. His strikes then become long, lancelike thrusts upstream to intercept the grasshopper, as far as twelve or fifteen feet from his waiting position, to which he returns after each strike.

As a result of this trout habit, the fly-fisherman who sees the riseform may overestimate the distance to the trout's position by at least fifteen feet. Add to this another five or six feet required for free float into the trout's suspected position, and the error amounts to twenty feet or more.

This error in judgment may cause the fisherman to approach too close to the trout's actual position, alarming him and putting him down for the rest of the day. I have seen this happen many times, and I too have committed the same error.

The only further advice I can offer is this: Walk softly and carry a big, salmon-size net.

Chapter Eight

Small Fly: Big Fish

It is a hot day in September, the season called the doldrums when the water is low and clear and the overhead sun makes the sweat run into your eyes. You have come to the quiet meadow stream to capture a big handsome trout, bull-shouldered from spring and summer feeding.

The bold, slashing trout strikes of spring have died with the big mayflies. The trout is now a furtive creature who makes leisurely, inconspicuous rises, sometimes so fleeting and insignificant as to be almost invisible. He is the smart trout of late summer and early fall, feeding on the millions of tiny insects that now crowd the stream.

In your hand you have the most graceful and delicate of modern sporting weapons: a light, dainty fly rod (preferably of split bamboo) that may weigh as little as one ounce. Brilliantly conceived and executed, the rod has the romantic appeal and appearance of an ancient Toledo blade, responsive to your slightest wish, nodding and trembling with every movement of your hand. Yet, it can be powerful, capable of hurling a long cast, and conquering a creature a hundred times its weight.

Attached to that rod there should be as fine a reel as you can afford, with tension adjustments and a silky smooth operation. You will depend heavily on this reel for the delicate give-and-take required to protect the leader's end, a fine strand called a tippet with a diameter as little as .0033 inch—as fine as human hair—and a breaking point of only three-quarters of a pound.

To the tip of that leader is attached a dry fly so tiny the complete rig is often referred to as "something invisible attached to nothing."

There is no precedent for this minute artificial. We inherited our angling techniques from an older generation devoted to larger dry flies, 12, 10, 8, even larger. No. 16 flies have long been considered "small" and No. 18, "tiny." But the flies for what I call "midge" fishing are much smaller—sizes 22, 24, 26, and 28. A No. 28 dry fly is to a No. 12 as a mosquito is to a large grasshopper.

One of my most exciting experiences with this sort of tackle was on a stifling day in late August. I prowled one of the long meadows of the beautiful Letort River near Carlisle, Pennsylvania, pausing now and then to cool off under a shady tree, but always looking keenly for some sign of a rise. Then I saw it, a faint wrinkle in the glassy surface that was gone in a flash. It happened on the outside edge of a little backwater near my bank.

Up to this point I had stayed well back from the water's edge,

looking from a safe distance (in smooth, clear water a trout can
see you at least thirty feet away when you stand at water level—
farther if you are on the bank). I knew I must avoid wading if
at all possible, so I began to stalk the fish on hands and knees.
Presently I could peer at him through streamside weeds from no
more than five or six feet.

That fish was magnificent, and when I got my first glimpse
of him I gasped a little. He was big-shouldered and heavy-
girthed, with a broad tail that undulated with easy power every
time he rose to take an insect. I estimated this brown trout to be
between three and four pounds and more than twenty inches
long. Every time he rose he drifted backward and lifted in that
languid manner that often characterizes a big trout. At the end
of each drift he turned away from me and faced the far bank as
he picked off the insect. The interval between rises was something like one minute.

I backed off until I was a safe distance from the water, then
sat down to ponder the situation and check my tackle. I peeled
off fifty feet of line and quickly respooled it to make sure there

were no kinks. My leader was a modern no-knot, continuous taper to 6X to which had been connected a thirty-inch tippet of 7X testing about one pound. After seeing the trout I promptly broke the 7X and replaced it with thirty inches of 6X, testing perhaps two pounds. I felt that I needed an extra margin of safety. (The no-knot leader is necessary on weed-filled streams like the Letort, as a conventional leader's several big knots pick and hold weed balls that are heavy enough to break a fine tippet.)

My rod was a seven-and-one-half foot, three-ounce bamboo on the stiff side. At that time of the year I needed length and stiffness to hold up my backcast above meadow weeds higher than my head. I tied on a No. 20 black beetle and hurried downstream to get below my fish, then approached the bank, crawling until I was about thirty feet below the trout.

Still crouched, I shook out the leader and some line to make sure everything was free and easy, then waited for the rise. Shortly it came and I marked its position in relation to a clump of grass on the bank. Now I began to extend line and leader until I had enough to make a pitch to the far bank, opposite the rise. Another pitch and shoot adjusted the length to put the fly two feet in front of the trout and a foot to his right, plus a float of at least six feet.

I slammed my pitch high and hard, deliberately overshooting so when the cast recoiled it came down just right, the loose, snaky 6X tippet settling softly on the surface. I could barely discern the little hump created by the tiny fly and noted with satisfaction it was floating freely on a true course. Now I saw the shadowy form of the trout beginning to lift, slowly undulating backward and upward, then turning to the right, and finally the little sip and the faint dimple on the surface.

The suspense created by the slow, deliberate, and visible rise of a big trout to your fly is agonizing. Only age and experience prevented me from jerking that fly from his open jaws or smashing the fine tippet with a violent strike.

Trembling, I lifted the rod gently and softly flexed the tip. Nothing happened and for a few long seconds time stood still. Suddenly the trout exploded in a furious dash upstream, plowing a long furrow in the water while my little reel chattered and whined. There were agonizing moments until he stopped short of a fallen willow. I looked down at my reel and noted with alarm that only a few turns of line were left on the drum, for I had no backing. (It would not have mattered anyway since there is no way to stop a big fish with midge tackle.)

I had put the rod tip down during that run and now I kept it low with the line hanging loosely. There was no pressure on the fish but he was still nervous, his head shaking in an effort to dislodge that passive but nagging irritation in his jaw.

Within a few minutes the trout became calm and I began the most delicate, tricky operation in midge fishing. I had to bring that fish back downstream, recover my line, and get him away from that fallen willow. One mistake and he would be into the willow with a jump.

I started by pinching the line with the thumb and forefinger of my free hand, drawing backward until I barely felt the fish. Then, increasing the pull slightly, I began to ease him toward me. I got him back a few feet before he realized what was happening to him. He got nervous again and I promptly released the line. When he had calmed I pinched the line and resumed; with several stops and starts, I got him back to his original position. But this was only the beginning.

I knew his kind—strong, wild, full of tricks. A smart trout that knew his ground better than I. His next maneuver was a familiar one that had lost me some fish in former years: He began swimming in a tight circle, slapping the leader hard with his tail. There is only one way to stop this—you must lift the rod high and parallel to the water, and with as much bend as possible.

When the trout found he could no longer slap the leader he became panicky, streaked downstream a short distance, turned

An occasional logjam in the path of a fleeing fish oftentimes spells disaster for the fisherman and his tackle.

upstream, and slithered into a big weed bed. I groaned. This is the safest refuge for a big meadow-stream trout and he knows it. It would be a grueling contest after all.

I hurried downstream to get below him, put the rod low and to one side with as much bend as possible short of breaking that 6X point. You cannot drag a big trout out of a weed bed; you must hold him with a light but constant downstream pressure until he tires and backs out of his own volition. Sometimes this takes many minutes. It worked for me on this occasion and the trout did what I expected—he ran downstream again and burrowed into another weed bed.

Through sweat-blurred eyes I suddenly noticed that one of the dreaded weed balls was draped over my leader. A weed ball the size of your fist is surprisingly heavy; it can pop a fine tippet if the fish moves before you can free the weeds. I hurried downstream below the resting fish, plunged my rod tip into the water to force the floating line below or at least level with the weed ball, and swished the rod tip from side to side. Soon I had the weed ball slipping toward me, pushed along by the current and the rod movement. I quickly removed it.

The dive-into-weeds maneuver was repeated over and over, each stop becoming a little shorter. The contest was going my way and I felt good about it until the trout suddenly bolted downstream and started around a bend. Between me and the fleeing trout was a swampy section that I could not negotiate. I ran backward and headed for high ground, the rod held high to clear the meadow weeds, and dashed in a circular route after the trout.

We arrived at the end of the bend neck and neck, the trout still racing. Now I saw a final hazard that I did not anticipate—a small, midstream logjam with a clear channel on both sides. If he headed through the far channel, all would be lost.

He headed for the far channel. There was hardly time to think and my next act was pure instinct. I lifted the rod high with a lot of line bellying from the tip, then drew the rod back

and hurled a high loop over the logjam. It cleared beautifully
and fell in the far channel, running freely with the trout down
the straightaway.

That was really the end of the fight. The trout's final defiant
gesture was to push his head into a patch of watercress near my
feet, leaving his body exposed. I netted him and carried him to a
clear, shallow channel near the bank, then sat down to stroke
him and help him recover.

What I said to this gallant fish during that rest period he
probably never understood. If he had, I am sure we would have
parted friends when, with a flick of his broad tail, he shot back
into the safety of the Letort—after a contest that had lasted an
hour and five minutes and had covered a quarter of a mile of
stream.

When an angler new to midge fishing sees me land a trout
like this, and I show him what I caught it on, the inevitable reaction is: "I don't believe it!" Not because the tackle is so delicate but because the fly is so tiny as to appear inconsequential.

Midge fishing differs from ordinary dry-fly fishing in two
ways. Instead of doing everything possible to make one of the
tiny flies float high by spraying it with a silicone solution and
carefully snapping the water droplets from it, the fly is cast *into
the surface film* so as to float flush like a drowning insect. This
is a radical departure from standard practice. Also, you must
never strike a fish in the conventional way with a sharp lift of
the rod.

The bite of the tiny hook is only about 1/16th of an inch,
microscopically enhanced by bending the hook so the point is
slightly offset to one side. As a result of this small bite, a midge
fly is tricky to lodge in a trout's mouth, as I relearned one day
last October when I located a really big trout feeding on tiny
Caenis flies. I watched as the old boy tipped up and down with
that easy, rocking-chair motion a big trout uses during a heavy
hatch.

After surveying the situation I decided that the only spot

The broken and sunken willow where the long contest nearly ended at the start.

Downstream—the distant limestone farmhouse where the contest with the big fish ended.

The tiny size #24 hooks can be very successfully used even with big fish. The only really good hold is in the tough tissue of the corner of the jaw. The fisherman cannot always have a choice but if he can, he should try to draw the hook from a position behind the fish. Drawing the hook across the bony sides or front of the jaws usually permits the hook to escape and the fish, too!

where I could pitch to him without causing the fly to drag was directly across from him. I didn't like this, but I had no choice. Eventually I got a good pitch in front of him that he took. I lifted the rod gently. The hook, a No. 24 on a one-pound tippet, held momentarily, then popped out of his jaws.

I renewed my casting. Again he took my little *Caenis.* I lifted as gently as before and again the hook came out. Bitterly disappointed, I sat there berating myself for botching it. Then, to my amazement, that big trout began to feed again.

I made a good pitch and watched breathlessly as he tipped and sucked the fly. For the third time, so help me, the little fly came out of his jaws. When I lifted the rod to make a fourth try I couldn't get the cast away; my hand shook and I had to let the cast die.

Curious now, I crossed the stream below the trout and came back up, crawling close to his position. What I saw startled me —he was a hook-billed male with a big gap in his jaws! The fly had merely scraped past his teeth.

You must get that little hook into the soft, tough tissue in the corner of a trout's mouth. Once embedded, the fly will stay there and nothing can shake it loose. To accomplish this you must cast either upstream or across at a fish that turns away on the take so the fly catches at the jaw hinge. Then all you need do is tighten the line gently to sink the barb.

What makes midge fishing exciting is the challenge and the variety; each trout stalked poses different problems. One trout last season seemed almost impregnable, since his lair was only a yard beyond a hot cattle fence.

Cows had cropped the grassy banks as close as a putting green and there was no cover. Yet there was this eighteen-incher sipping *Caenis* spinners and there was that dreadful fence. I knew the trout would bolt downstream under the fence the moment he felt the hook.

I made a desperate plan. I put my landing net on the bank near a large bed of watercress. Then I crawled under the fence well away from the stream and inched toward it, pulling myself along by my elbows.

In position at last and still prone, I raised my right arm and cast. The trout took and shot under the fence. Keeping the rod low, I lurched up and ran to the fence and poked the throbbing rod under it. I was just able to reach across the fence and grab the rod with my other hand. Then I hurled the rod at the watercress thirty feet downstream.

Again I crawled under the fence. When I had dashed to the watercress and retrieved my rod, the trout was still on. I picked up my net, for the campaign was won. Some say trout fishing is a contemplative sport, but it never is when you stick a tiny fly into a big unsuspecting trout.

Part Three

TROUT
RIVERS
IN
PROFILE

Anatomy of the Limestone
and Freestone Trout Waters

IN THE EARLY HOURS OF THE GEOLOGIC TIME CLOCK, SPANNING MIL-
lions of years, the earth was covered with a gaseous atmosphere
and warm, shallow seas that were constantly lashed by electrical
and rain storms from above and battered by countless exploding
volcanoes from below. More millions of years passed, during
which the hardening surface convulsed and buckled from time
to time raising some landmasses out of the seas, dropping
others below the surface. These seas were rich with nutrients;
they contained the chemistry of life out of which the first form-
less cell colonies began to appear.

Eventually the cell colonies began to specialize and finally many of these early sea creatures acquired shell-like coverings. They were soft-bodied animals that carried their skeletons on the outside rather than the inside as we do. There was one large class of these creatures, belonging to the order Foraminifera, especially important to future mankind generally and to fishermen in particular. They were extremely tiny creatures with shells that were perforated with many small holes through which they extended tiny flexible arms. The early seas swarmed with the little animals. They were short-lived and after death fell in a constant shower to the bottom of the sea, eventually building up to a great depth. How deeply did they accumulate in a single year? No one knows, perhaps a half inch or an inch accumulated yearly over a period of millions of years until they measured thousands of feet thick.

The earth's crust continued to change, buckling, infolding, raising mountains, expelling the seas, burying the great layer of dead animals under a burden of rubble, sand, volcanic rocks, and other materials. Thus, burdened and pressured, the entombed bodies were compacted to a hard rock that we describe today as limestone. A great deal of it all around the earth was formed in this way. Some of it was also formed by chemical precipitation as a kind of mud in the bottom of the sea that was eventually pressured and hardened into limestone. In some areas of the earth these processes were repeated several times so that there may be in those areas several deep layers, deposited by successive seas.

The creation of limestone has never really stopped. In many parts of the oceans the little sea creatures are constantly building coral reefs and islands with their bodies, all of which is basically calcium carbonate and could eventually end up as dense limestone or marble, which is also limestone in a crystalline form.

Out of all this has come the most valuable and useful building material that the civilized world has ever known. In the limestone country of Pennsylvania, you can see the many fine barns, homes, and magnificent churches built with cut limestone blocks. Limestone is burnt to make cement with which great buildings, bridges, dams, and a vast highway system are built all over the world. Limestone by means of various processes is used for medicines and the precious fertilizers needed to grow food for man and animals. It is no exaggeration to say that the entire civilized world is resting or riding on the backs of the tiny foraminifers, sea creatures so small that forty or fifty thousand of them may be compacted in one cubic inch of limestone.

There are no statues erected to honor this little animal, no speeches to eulogize it, no poems to glorify it—all of which has been done for lesser and less deserving creatures, whose contributions to mankind do not begin to measure up to the enormous benefits that I have mentioned.

There is one more benefit that I must mention, one that is important to many of us as fishermen—namely, the existence of the wonderful limestone streams and rivers, different in significant ways from freestone rivers.

The birth of the limestoners took place some five or six hundred million years ago after the limestone beds were laid and buried in the earth followed by the expulsion of the seas and the elevation of the present landmasses. Then the rainfall, sinking through the porous earth, eventually found its way into fissures, cracks, or faults in the hard limestone and began to erode and enlarge these fissures, pursuing the dip and strike of the rock beds and thus forming numerous solution channels; many of these became interconnected, many of them enlarged enormously to become such gigantic caverns as the Mammoth cave in Kentucky, the Carlsbad in New Mexico, and other famous ones with hundreds of miles of underground rivers, lakes, waterfalls, galleries, avenues, and domed rooms so large that they would hold a Gothic cathedral. There is good reason to believe that there are many such caverns as yet undiscovered.

A limestone stream, a limestone barn, and a limestone fisherman belong together in the Pennsylvania Dutch country.

This vast subterranean system of watercourses, the extent of which no man knows, is a great reservoir; it is the unfailing source of supply for the surface limestone rivers.

Water, of course, will not run uphill. The limestoners as a general rule issue from faults or cracks at low elevations and the water that you see at the source of the stream, erroneously called springs, is only the top of the great sunken reservoir spilling over a little at the surface of the earth. The water that you see is only a very tiny portion of that reservoir and it is like seeing only the tip of a gigantic iceberg. Actually, these surface rivers are brief exposures of hidden underground rivers pursuing their leisurely, solitary courses in the lowlands to join another river or, as often happens, to disappear and go back into the earth through one of the numerous sinkholes that exist in the limestone country; sometimes the same river reappears through another fault or crack in the rocks many miles away.

A freestone river is usually formed in high elevations, deriving its waters from melting snows and ice fields and from numerous true springs or pockets of water that issue in trickles to join with other trickles and form larger waterways as they move downhill. They are far more dependent on new rainfall for volume than the limestoners. That same dependency often results in periodical floods and raging torrents that denude the rivers of organic life and cause great damage to everything in the path of the rushing water. In times of low rainfall or drought, the freestoners become low and stagnant, with increasingly high temperatures inimical to the existence of some fish and insect life. In winter, they often form anchor ice or stream bottom ice that traps and suffocates many forms of fish and insect life.

Thus, we arrive at one of the really great differences between limestone and freestone rivers, and that is the matter of stability. That is one of the two great virtues of the limestoners. It means specifically a constancy of volume, freedom from violent disruptions to flora and fauna (except in very rare instances), and maintenance of the proper temperatures. The latter is particularly valuable for cold-water fish life, and occurs because the rivers issue from the caverns consistently at 47 to 56 degrees; their great volume sustains the influence of these temperatures, thus delaying excessive and harmful heating of the water for many miles, especially if there are additional faults or cracks to permit the junction with more underground rivers. In this way the limestoners do not form ice in wintertime for a great distance below their outlets because the water is actually warmer than air, even though the air may be well below the freezing point. In summer these waters remain adequately cool no matter what the air temperature may be.

All this is much more apparent today than it was a hundred years ago when the eastern half of the United States was canopied with a vast forest into which the sun never penetrated. It is a truly strange experience to walk through a primeval forest— silent, cathedral-like, softly lighted, with a deep spongy turf that muffles every footfall. That deep spongy forest carpet was the real treasure of the freestoners. It was both a reservoir and a thermostat that held the rainfall in reserve, cooling it and letting it out slowly into the rivers; this provided the only source of stability available.

That fine reservoir was destroyed by the pioneer and lumberman who denuded the eastern half of the United States of its great forests, exposing the forest floor to sun and wind, after which it caught fire and burned over many thousands of square miles leaving only the bare bones of the earth.

A freestoner cannot survive civilization, a limestoner can.

Now we come to the second of the two great differences between limestone and freestone, namely, fertility.

Limestone is composed principally of calcium carbonate, which is expressed by the symbol $CaCO_3$. It is the calcium and sometimes magnesium dissolved in the water that makes water "hard," something not much appreciated by the housewife because soap doesn't lather well, reacting instead and forming curds and making all kinds of washing unsatisfactory. These

The beautiful valley of the Tulpehocken.

constituents along with other nutrients are the fertilizers that stimulate the plant growth that starts the entire food chain, beginning with the microscopic animal and vegetable planktons all the way up to the huge weed beds often seen in the limestoners. The water plants not only provide food and cover but also produce oxygen, without which underwater life could not survive. These plants are especially important to the quiet meadow streams that do not tumble about and absorb oxygen from the air.

The plant community in the limestoners is often varied but is always typical of alkaline-loving species—watercress, chara, duckweed, elodea, and others. Highly alkaline waters are easily identified by these plants. They fit very well into the entire limestone system. The constituents of limestone, eroded and carried to the surface waters from the bowels of the earth, are dissolved by the carbonic acid (H_2CO_3) that is created by carbon dioxide reacting with water. The dissolution of these constitu-

A typical freestone river.

ents forms soluble carbonates and bicarbonates. It is the peculiar ability of these particular alkaline-loving plants to convert bicarbonate to free carbon dioxide in their cells in the process of photosynthesis, which takes place when living plants are exposed to sunlight, thus creating the vital oxygen for bacteria and other living organisms in the water. The bacteria in turn utilize the oxygen to decompose dead plants and animals, reducing them to useful nutrients, phosphates, and nitrates that are absorbed for growth by living plants along with more carbon dioxide respired by living bacteria and animals. The limestoners actually benefited by the removal of forests on their banks in the early days; this let in the sunlight, which triggered the photosynthetic process. Today, with the massive influx of pollutants causing excessive weed growth and excessive decomposition, it might be a good thing to replant the trees along the banks to cut off the sunlight, to limit the weed growth, and create a better balance.

The soft acid waters of the freestoners do not have this valuable carbonate system. These are primarily surface waters flowing around and over rocks of volcanic origin—the sandstones, quartzites, and granitic types that do not contain organic material and probably never did. These waters are often tainted with humic or tannic acid leached out of the hillsides by periodic rainfall.

The question is sometimes raised as to whether or not the freestoners can be helped in some way to increase their fertility. I think so. Fertility could be increased cheaply and efficiently by dumping some truckloads of crushed limestone into the fast riffle areas, and in the sterile, infertile waters, by the addition of a bit of pollution perhaps in the form of animal manure in perforated containers in order to supply bacteria and decomposed vegetable matter; this is exactly what we do to our gardens to make them flourish. The judicious application of some dams or retarders in streams of steep gradient would help in the formation of silt beds to hold plant life, which is ordinarily very meager in freestoners.

This is not unreasonable when you realize that many free-stoners become limestoners by the infusion of dissolved lime salts from pure limestone tributaries. A classic example of this is the famed Yellow Breeches, which starts in the south mountains of the Blue Ridge Chain as a freestoner, then drops into the Cumberland Valley to be joined by a number of pure lime-stoners, thus raising the alkalinity and enormously enriching this trout river.

The richness of a limestoner with a high alkaline rating (pH of more than 7) will tax your credibility. Many years ago when I was actively investigating the potential of the limestone waters, particularly in the weedy places, I did some sampling by blocking off one-square-foot areas of weed, which I removed and carefully sifted for fish food. In every instance I found the typical hard water animals in astonishing abundance, especially in the beds of callitriche and watercress. Always there were great numbers of sow bugs, beetles, scuds, snails, nymphs, and one or two larger food forms. Some of these samplings revealed a food supply of five thousand pounds per acre (wet weight) and this did not include bottom organisms from the silt or mud. In each instance I got a lump of small insects plus at least one larger animal like a crayfish or minnow or sculpin, the whole of which usually weighed from one and a half to two ounces. On the basis of 43,560 square feet per acre, this yield was remark-ably high. Compare this with many freestoners flowing down steep gradients over hardpan that will not yield ten pounds of fish food per acre.

The growth rate in alkaline waters can be phenomenal, as much as six inches a year, which compares well with hatchery fish. Scale readings of one brown trout caught when he weighed fifteen pounds indicated that he was a little over eight years old. Atlantic salmon can get that big in about half that time but a salmon has the enormous expanse of food-rich alka-line seas within which to roam and grow fat. Anyone must admit that fifteen pounds in eight years is a mighty good per-formance for a little limestoner that could be spanned from bank to bank by a first-class broad jumper. This is not unusual in these small Pennsylvania limestones. Many freestoners cannot grow a trout more than six inches long or more than a quarter of a pound in weight in his entire lifetime.

Awareness and knowledge of these great differences between limestone and freestone rivers did not generally exist among fishermen until recent years. These distinctions existed only among the limnologists and water biologists. Twenty-five years ago the late Edward Ringwood Hewitt, famed fisherman, author, fish culturist, scientist, and a widely traveled person, wrote and published a review of my findings on limestone trout streams. His review included the following comment: "It is unfortunate that we have so few streams (limestone) of this type in the United States. I know of about a dozen in Pennsylvania and one in Maryland, one in northern Ohio, and two in Idaho." This was a surprising statement coming from a man who had fished extensively in the Far West, particularly Yellowstone Park, in the late 1800s, where limestoners are numerous. In the West they are called spring creeks and are now much sought and heavily fished by thousands, especially in Montana, Wyoming, and Idaho. Anyone who has traveled through Yellowstone Park must have seen the gray substance piled up around the blowholes of the geysers and hot springs. That material is mostly calcium carbonate—the foodstuff of the limestoners. There are some fine alkaline waters in the Midwest and perhaps the best of these is the famous Au Sable system in the lower peninsula of Michigan. Wisconsin has them too. In Pennsylvania I have fished at least twenty such rivers. They can be found in all sections of the United States except the New England states and New York, where there is only one as far as I know.

I do not say that freestoners cannot provide good fishing or grow big fish. They can—or I should say, they did at one time. Old records prove this but that was back in a day when trout were not caught out so fast and had time to grow. Big freestone trout come from big rivers, not from little ones.

A big freestone river will not produce more food per acre than a small one but it will produce more food by sheer weight because of its greater area in which a big trout can roam and find enough of it. And even though the freestoners do not have the valuable carbonate system, they have a source of nutrients in the form of fallen leaves, sunken trees, and other organic items that decompose and provide the support for useful algae and plankton to start the food chain; still, much of this was and is often swept away by periodic floods, preventing a stable population in plant and animal, and requiring a new start each time.

In my state of Pennsylvania there are five counties in the north tier that contain at least a thousand miles of what were once magnificent freestone trout rivers. We know how good they were because we have a fine record about these rivers in a rare and fascinating little book called *The Vanishing Trout* by Charles Lose, an educated and observant man who fished these waters when they were unspoiled. Just think of making a catch of fifteen native brook trout, three of which, together, weighed more than nine pounds. Those were the glory days of the freestoners.

The brook trout is well adapted to acid waters and is believed to be the finest product of the freestoners by many eastern fishermen who constitute a special cult that won't acknowledge the excellence of any other kind of trout fishing. It does no good to tell them that the brook trout is not a real trout but a char. They would merely shrug and say that it was the bad luck of real trout not to become char. The affection that many easterners have for the brook trout is remarkable. As a boy, which was quite some time ago, I remember with what reverence and admiration a seventeen-inch wild brook trout was regarded by the citizens who gathered often at the village firehouse. The man who caught the trout achieved a respectful acclaim that he never earned in any other way. That incident happened fifty

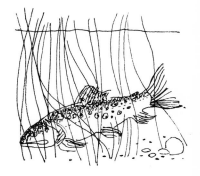

years ago. Recently, on a visit there I met the man who caught that seventeen-incher—and he was still talking about it!

This affection goes beyond reason and is really very difficult to explain. Some years ago I had a friend, now deceased, who was one of the most avid fishermen that I have ever met. He sought and found every kind of worthwhile rod-fishing on this earth and what's more he could afford it. He was familiar with the best of Atlantic salmon fishing, the swordfishing at Acapulco, bonefishing in the South, the big rainbows of the Northwest, the big perch of the Nile, and a lot of other fishing about which I know nothing. On one occasion when we were on a fishing trip together, we just sat and talked for a while, exchanging ideas, philosophies, and reminiscing as fishermen often do. During the course of the conversation I asked him to tell me what his finest fishing experience was. He astonished me. Instead of some exotic adventure in some foreign land as I expected, he began to relate with great relish a day's fishing that he had, fishing for wild brook trout in a small freestone stream not many miles from our homes. This was not a passing fancy with this man. He had, many years before, commissioned a famous rod-builder to make him a tiny rod for this kind of fishing, even before midge rods were named as such.

I have to confess that I too have a great affection for the American brook trout and the picturesque freestoners. The first trout that I caught was a real northern "hemlock" trout taken on a wet Grey Hackle Red and not a dry fly as you might think. I remember with what awe and astonishment I looked at the jewellike beauty of that very handsome creature and later when I came to the limestone country I caught many more brook trout than brown or rainbow trout. The limestoners had them in a great quantity, and big ones too, but I did not fish for them in an earlier time when they averaged two pounds in weight, according to available records. Even now, when my trout fishing is almost exclusively for brown and rainbow trout, I welcome any opportunity to fish for brook trout, not in stocked waters containing those pale, insipid-looking hatchery fish but in some remote area as yet not completely spoiled by mankind. I know of a few such places.

I have some good memories of wonderful days with brook trout. On one occasion in the far north country I was fishing for Atlantic salmon on a famous river. The fishing was extremely poor, as salmon fishing often is, and while others groused and complained I set about to find some other kind of fishing in that area. I inquired here and there among the natives and eventually I was directed to a backcountry road not far from my lodging where a small run of peaty-looking water flowed under the little bridge that spanned the road. It was not very impressive but I left the road and walked back into the gloom of the heavily timbered area. What a transformation I saw! The little stream ran over clean, bright gravel, sometimes in little quiet pools, with an occasional shaft of sunlight playing on its surface, sometimes running down a gentle riffle, quarreling and talking to itself, sometimes dropping in miniature waterfalls. It was quiet, pleasant walking on the untrampled spongy turf. Nowhere was there any sign of fishing pressure. I was glad that I had remembered to bring a small trout rod with me and some trout flies as well. I had a glorious afternoon with those little brook trout. I caught so many that I lost count but every one of them was an exciting event. Food is scarce in those acid peaty waters of the North, so anything that looks edible is the object of a violent slashing attack. I can imagine the thinking of one of those little fellows when a juicy-looking fly is coming his way. "Ha!" he thinks, "this is where I eat again this week."

The resultant strike by a little seven- or eight-incher actually jars your hand very noticeably. I remember in particular one monster that was all of ten inches long. I saw him in a sun-dappled little pool with no other occupant in it. I had been fishing small wet flies but now I switched to a dry because there was room here to make a backcast. I pitched a tiny Adams in front of him. He backed downstream watching intently, fins fanning furiously, then he struck and in that confined space, no bigger than a washtub, it became the stage for a titanic struggle. I landed him, handled him as gently as possible, then released him. When I left he looked fine, a little dejected perhaps, but I think he enjoyed that experience as much as I did. When I returned home from that distant and expensive fishing trip, did I bring back unforgettable memories of battling big fresh-run Atlantic salmon? Not so. The unforgettable memory was that of a ten-inch monster brook trout and the Lilliputian battle in that sun-dappled pool.

Chapter Ten

The Au Sable

I CANNOT THINK OR WRITE ABOUT MICHIGAN'S FAMED AU SABLE River without using superlative terms. Dr. Hazen L. Miller, author of a fascinating book, *The Old Au Sable*, 1966, called it a study in amity, and further described it as one of the most amiable of rivers, with only a few exceptions, its residents are friendly. I could not have said it better—neither more accurately nor more concisely.

Of all the big rivers I have fished none are friendlier or kinder to the fisherman. It is the most easily waded river that I know, requiring neither chains, nor felt shoes, nor wading staff. Only rarely does a wading fisherman encounter a small greasy slick or patch of clay on the beautifully clean sandy, gravelly bottom. Even the elderly wade and fish with pleasure in it. The river's kindliness is even better explained by the fact that never in its recorded history has it created any kind of a damaging flood. Its depth is remarkably uniform throughout its entire length. A brief rise of the water level in the spring is barely perceptible, quickly settling back to its stable, normal level. Moreover, this is a river on which the fly-fisherman can rely unreservedly for clear, unsullied waters on the opening day of trout season, at the end of April. Moved by a powerful curiosity to learn about the Au Sable, I did a considerable amount of investigation, uncovering facts which explain why this is one of the unique rivers of the world.

The Au Sable River is located in the Lower Michigan Peninsula. The main branch begins at the junction of Kolke Creek and Bradford Creek in the northwest part of the Au Sable River basin in Crawford County. It meanders southward to Grayling where it is joined by the east branch, extending from Lake Saint Helen, through Roscommon to join the main stream in western Crawford County along with the north branch which has its source in Otsego County. The main river then continues eastward through Oscoda, Alcona, and Iosco counties, emptying into Lake Huron at Oscoda.

It is a tremendous system of trout rivers which drains approximately 1,800 square miles of the area. This system lies in a comparatively level land area; a gradient of only five feet to the mile, accounting for the gentility and smoothness of the river currents.

The most important element that contributes to the character of these rivers is the composition of the soil through which this river flows. The principal overlay in this area is a very deep deposit of coarse sand undoubtedly left there by ancient inland

The Au Sable, in Michigan's Lower Peninsula, is one of the world's unique rivers. Its incredibly food-rich waters support an enormous population of trout.

seas and retreating glaciers. It is really a desert wasteland that broke the hearts of early settlers who tried to cultivate and farm the inhospitable soil. Numerous abandoned farms attest to the despair of a people who could lick the Indians but not the land. It is this sandy overlay that makes the Au Sable the superb river it is. Heavy rainfalls and the melting of deep snows that characterize this region are immediately absorbed into the soil and percolate downward very deeply to a hard, impervious lower stratum, thence the water trickles laterally toward the banks and empties into the river in the form of innumerable springs, some of them exposed, many others hidden. It is a curious sensation to walk the soft, springy turf, beneath the covering cedars along the banks and hear the murmuring waters underfoot, but not seeing them. This inexhaustible reserve of well-filtered, cool, clear water is the prime reason for the Au Sable's constancy of flow, its purity and its clearness. Not a drop of water is wasted in this country. None of it is dissipated in the form of freshets, floods, or standing puddles. The blottering effect of the sandy terrain promptly seizes and treasures every bit of water that falls.

If I must make comparisons, then I will say that the only rivers on earth comparable to the Au Sable are the fabled chalk streams of England. The limestones of Pennsylvania and the Far West are often likened to the chalk streams and it is true that they are similar in chemistry, the richness of weed life, abundance of insects, and the ability to grow numerous fine trout. The Au Sable has all this but more closely approaches the nature of an English chalk stream because of the manner of its creation and maintenance. The chalky downs of southern England composed of a soft, porous, highly absorbent material accept and hoard every bit of rainfall, releasing it slowly in the form of well-filtered, cool, pure spring water; exactly as such water is delivered to the Au Sable.

On the score of productivity, you do not need a professional analysis to see that it is one of the earth's richest trout streams.

Typical flora and fauna of the hard alkaline waters exist everywhere. In the shallows of the main river and the branches that I fished—north and south—I saw an enormous number of wild baby trout indicating ideal spawning and hatching conditions. Aquatic insect life is unbelievably abundant. Justin and Fannie Leonard, Michigan entomologists, report that a one-foot bottom sample from a gravel area in the north branch of the Au Sable contained 1,374 nymphs; 1,277 of them were specimens of *Ephemerella invaria* and *subvaria*, more commonly known as light and dark Hendricksons. This is an incredible yield and nothing that I know of among the Pennsylvania limestones or elsewhere is any richer.

There are four distinct phases during the year when fly-fishing is at its best. Phase one occurs in early season when the trout are especially ravenous after their long winter fast. Stonefly, caddis fly, and mayfly hatches occur daily during this period, which may last for a month from opening day. The most spectacular of them is the stupendous hatch of Hendricksons that issues at this time. Michigan people commonly describe it as a blanket hatch, a term that certainly applies, as I can attest, for I have often seen the river blanketed from bank to bank with this big beautiful mayfly. As anyone knows who has fished during this kind of a hatch, it is not easy to catch trout even though many thousands of them may be rising all over the river. You need to cast accurately, rapidly, and particularly to watch for a patch of open water, devoid of naturals, and make a timely pitch with your artificial in order to get the attention of the trout.

All these early season hatches are daytime hatches. The Hendrickson often begins to hatch in the forenoon and once it begins it does not quit until nightfall. Occasionally, there are brief lulls during the day when the hatch slackens off and the feeding is interrupted for a short period. I am always mighty glad for these brief rest periods, grasping at every opportunity to rest my weary casting arm. No matter how tired you may be, when the hatch resumes, you will joyfully drag yourself back to your feet and fling your flies about with a renewed enthusiasm. If your visit is long enough and you are lucky enough to be present when the Hendrickson spinners begin to come back to lay their eggs and fall on the water in great numbers, your long daytime fishing, exhausting enough, will extend far into the gloom of nightfall and you will be forced to call on hidden reserves of energy to meet this contingency. The frenzied feeding on spinners is enough to unravel the composure of the most seasoned fisherman, often leaving him with a deep feeling of frustration, when finally he is forced to break off at the end of the spinner fall.

The second important phase starts about May 20 and continues until mid-June with the emergence of the Brown Drake (*E. simulans*), which issues sporadically during the day but emerging heavily from dusk until midnight. The hatches and rise of trout are especially good on the north and south branches of the Au Sable, with peak emergence lasting for about five days on any of the branches. This phase really must be classed as nighttime fishing, something that is regarded with distaste by many fishermen, but if you are looking for excitement and big trout, the Brown Drake will provide both. Fishing in the dark on these waters is feasible because of the easy wading I mentioned earlier. Nevertheless, it is a good plan to choose a productive area of water and examine it closely in the daytime for any wading hazards, room for backcasts, and ease of maneuvering. Michigan fishermen tell many wonderful stories about night-shrouded battles with big trout accompanied by many popped leaders and lost flies.

The third phase is undoubtedly the highlight of the year. This involves the King of Michigan mayflies, in what is known famously as the "caddis" hatch. It is not a caddis at all, as everyone knows, but is really the big mayfly, *Hexagenia limbata*, a far more dramatic creature than even the Brown Drake. It is a well-distributed insect inhabiting other Michigan rivers, notably the Boardman and Pere Marquette. The huge nymphs, known as "wigglers," have considerable commercial value to many enterprising individuals who make a profitable business of collecting and selling them to ice fishermen during the winter months. These big nymphs may run as many as five hundred to the square foot of stream bottom.

The sizes and buzzardlike proportions of the artificials used for this hatch by fishermen are appalling, oftentimes as large as size 4!

That hatch usually begins in the second or third week in June, extending to mid-July and, like the Brown Drake, commences to emerge at dusk, about 9 o'clock, continuing heavily until midnight. The mating flight of the spinners, an awesome sight, takes place between dusk and midnight, a day or two following emergence. They swarm like a blizzard for miles up and down the course of the stream heralded by the rustling, rushing sound of furiously beating wings. This, too, is primarily night-time fishing but many fishermen find it profitable to fish in the early dawn hours for large trout that are lingering and looking for another taste of the big succulent mayfly.

The fourth phase is much more obscure and not nearly so spectacular as the first three but in the opinion of many it is the best, the most interesting, and fascinating. It is the small fly period in mid and late summer and includes the terrestrial insects as well as the aquatics. Michigan fishermen lump them all together and describe them as midges or midge fishing. Actually, all these small flies represent phases within a phase. One of the surprising discoveries to me is the marvelous fishing accruing from the *Caenis* hatch, reportedly as good as it exists in Pennsylvania. Additionally, Michigan fly-fishermen have learned, like Pennsylvanians, that there is a superlative kind of fishing to be enjoyed with the terrestrial patterns: the jassids, ants, beetles, and particularly the grasshopper on the western side of the lower peninsula.

I have emphasized the four phases but that is not to say that

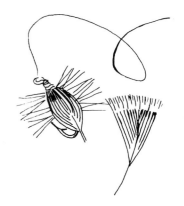

the fisherman is thereby limited. No, indeed! The fishing year on the Au Sable system is one continuous round of hatches, land-bred and water-born.

No discussion of the Au Sable would be adequate without reference to the unique methods employed in fishing this unique water. Here again the physical character of the river enters into our calculations.

Ages ago the Au Sable began to cut its way through the impacted, sandy, gravelly terrain until it hit bedrock, leaving steeply sloping, blufflike formations on both banks. These banks are thickly grown with Michigan or western white cedars, which periodically are loosened at the roots by the persistent action of the currents, and are toppled into the river. At one time, prior to the settlement of this area, the whole river was choked with this debris, the tips of the tall cedars meeting at midstream and interlocking to form an impenetrable barrier to river traffic. Early settlers called these fallen cedars "sweepers," just as they are called today. Then, in the middle and late nineteenth century, the lumbermen came and cut back the "sweepers" from the center of the river to permit the passage of logs. Still later in modern times, the "sweepers" have been further cut and controlled by the owners of canoe liveries who cater to the numerous vacationers who like to make float trips down the Au Sable and its branches. I have heard complaints from fishermen who bemoan the interference of the canoe traffic during the fishing season but frankly, in the years that I have fished the Au Sable, I have not seen any evidence to prove that the canoeists hurt the fishing at all. The trout continue to rise, no matter how many canoes pass. On one occasion only did I suffer any discomfort because of a canoe. Actually, the trouble was caused by two canoes, joined together like a catamaran. I was fishing in a rather narrow stretch of the river, concentrating on a good rise of trout to the Hendrickson, when I heard a noise behind me. I turned and was startled to see a

double canoe rig, bearing down on me very rapidly and entirely spanning the current in which I was standing. It was a case of either fight or jump. The occupants of the double canoe rig thought it was great fun! All I could do was to hurl a bit of colorful language after them to alleviate my feelings somewhat.

I do urge those liverymen to eliminate or at least discourage the use of that frightful double canoe rig.

Let us get back to the "sweepers"—those dreadful but wonderful "sweepers." Everybody agrees that without them there would not be the vast trout population that occupies the Au Sable. Nearly all the trout are contained in that awful tangle of fallen cedars for many miles along the banks. Everybody stands in the middle of the river and fishes toward the "sweepers," pecking away at the little bays and pockets and the outer or nearest edges of the cedar trunks. There are many thousands of trout hidden in the "sweepers" that grow old and die and never come close to feeling the prick of a hook or lure of any kind.

For a long time I accepted this dictum and practice. Then one day I sat on a log and watched with growing impatience and annoyance the activities of several big trout feeding on the Hendricksons that drifted and trickled into the protected recesses of the cedar tangle. I laid aside the rod and labored mightily to pull and tug at branches, twigs, trunks, and ancient roots. Finally, I achieved a cleared area to which I could make a cast. I sat and waited a long time until confidence was restored to the trout and feeding was resumed. I chose the biggest trout, made a good pitch, and had the satisfaction of seeing him tip up and gently suck in my artificial. Imagine my dismay when, after setting the hook, my leader came streaking toward me along with the blurred form of a big trout diving into the debris near my feet. I was promptly smashed. Thoroughly humbled by this experience and, like any other sensible Au Sable fisherman, I went back to pecking away at little bays and pockets and the edges of things from the middle of the river.

Two views of the famed and dreaded "sweepers" that line the riverbanks. They are credited with the river's tremendous trout population. A high degree of skill is required to fish the "sweepers" successfully. The rewards, however, can be great.

How productive is the Au Sable fishing? The really big trout are caught during the phase two and three periods. The early season hatches and fishing do not yield the bigger trout. I like the early season fishing because of the daytime hatches and the numerous trout that feed on the surface. It can be spectacular. It is possible and happens very frequently that a diligent fisherman either by boat or on foot can raise, scratch, hook, roll, and catch fifty to a hundred trout in a day's fishing. The ratio of trout caught to those raised is sometimes poor because of the necessity for making downstream casts into the slanting "sweepers." Striking upstream against the hard, bony front edge of a trout's mouth often results in a failure to hook him. But the action is constant and exciting and sometimes you have an unforgettable day when everything is working just right.

On one occasion back in the spring of 1966 I was out with Art Neumann who fished with me until midafternoon, when he wandered off to some other part of the river and left me alone on a very beautiful stretch of the main river. Up to that point the fishing had been rather slow. Then I began to notice an unusual amount of activity by numerous birds, mostly swallows, swooping and darting about, obviously intercepting and seizing insects in midair. It did not take me long to discover that the Hendrickson spinners were swarming over the river preparatory to mating and egg laying. It was an old familiar pattern and I knew immediately that I was in for a big evening. The Hendrickson spinner is probably the most obliging of all mayfly species, issuing and falling earlier than most other mayfly spinners. This fall was even earlier than usual, promising a great deal of daylight fishing. And so it happened. Best of all, the fall of spinners was gradual and sparse at any given moment so that there was no great concentration of naturals to offer competition to my artificial. The trout responded nobly.

It seemed that every trout in the river was out looking for spinners, and every one of them good, heavy trout—bigger than usual in early season. It required only one or two accurate pitches to any trout, who promptly seized the artificial and tore downriver peeling off line at an alarming rate, forcing me to pursue him in order to hold my reserve line. There was only one cleared area below me among the sweepers where I could beach any of them. I had to follow and fight every one of those trout into that beach, land and release him, then plow my way back upriver to that long riffle where the trout were rising furiously. After each return to the riffle it required only a few false casts and a single pitch to any trout and away we would go downriver again. Each return left me breathless until it seemed that I could never get enough air to breathe. When it ended at dusk I was thoroughly wilted and my feet hurt from slamming my toes repeatedly against loose-fitting waders during my frequent runs downriver. Understandably, I was oblivious to everything else around me during all this fury and did not know or realize that Art had returned and had been standing on the bank for some time watching with amazement this whole crazy performance. On the last day of our trip four of us had a closely similar experience with the spinner and a good rise of trout, which ripped and tore my favorite spinner pattern to shreds, until there was hardly anything left but a bare hook. This is the sort of thing that you can expect from the Au Sable.

Many visitors to the Au Sable prefer to fish on foot but many others like to fish from the famed Au Sable riverboat, the most unusual freshwater craft that I have ever seen. It had its origin sometime in the middle of the last century and, as nearly as I can determine, was first mentioned and described in print by Thaddeus Norris, a hallowed name in American fishing annals. Norris wrote extensively about the marvelous grayling fishing, now regrettably extinct in Michigan, that he first experienced—in 1874. Much of his fishing was done from the now familiar Au Sable riverboat, and his description fits very accurately the boat that is used today except for length. Norris's boat was sixteen feet long. Today's boat exceeds twenty feet and may be as much as twenty-four feet. Originally, it was made of white pine but now it is made of cedar or plywood, often reinforced with a fiber-glass sheathing on the bottom.

Invention and design of the boat is credited to I. F. Babbitt, member of an early Grayling family, and also to one Ed Augur, another Grayling resident. In any event, it is a boat that rivals, in elegance and grace, the loveliest of all small craft, the Indian birchbark canoe.

It is essentially a two-man boat. Then, as now, it was built with a raised live-box just a few feet behind the bow on which the forward angler sits. The live-box is watertight above the flooring but has heavy screening underneath to admit the circulating water in order to keep the fish alive. It is a common practice to return alive and unhurt the smaller trout and replace them with larger fish as they are caught during the course of a float trip. Altogether, the Au Sable riverboat is a sleek, trim affair—a mere sliver of a boat, drawing only two or three inches of water and having no more than a handspan of freeboard.

It is an extremely entertaining sight to behold the skill with which the stern occupant maneuvers with his single pole grasped in one hand with one end of the pole tucked under an armpit, the other hand simultaneously wielding a fly rod with amazing dexterity. With that one-handed pole the boatman can back and fill—drift and stop—sometimes holding his boat motionless and slantwise to the current while he and his guest make quick, accurate throws to the edge of the "sweepers" where the trout are hidden.

One of the principal reasons for the boat's ease of maneuverability is the fact that all of them drag a short length of heavy chain, which acts as a kind of slipping anchor and/or dragging rudder. The weight and length of the chain is carefully adjusted to each boat to permit only a very slow free drift with the bow pointed downstream. Only the remarkably stable level and flow of the Au Sable could make this kind of an arrangement work successfully, day in and day out, season after season.

The famed Au Sable riverboat rivals in elegance and grace the Indian birchbark canoe. Many anglers prefer to fish the river from this craft.

Thus far I have discussed only the first part of Dr. Miller's fine prescription. The second part, "Its people are friendly," deserves recall that I have never met a more hospitable group of residents or fishermen than I found in Michigan's Lower Peninsula, all the way from Saginaw to the hintermost parts of the Au Sable Basin. Nevertheless, even with all that courtesy and hospitality (they may even allow you the first bite in a dispute), they know how to resent an offense or unsportsmanlike behavior. Every stranger is initially welcomed. Thereafter he will be carefully observed for any sign of impropriety and eventually he will learn in many subtle ways whether or not he has been approved. These people love their fine river. They may forgive a personal offense but not one to their river.

You cannot fish the Au Sable very long before you realize that you are being unofficially hosted by the big, influential Trout Unlimited organization. There are signs of this everywhere. The Au Sable system is the special darling—the special concern—of all T.U. members in Michigan. Together with an enlightened and progressive Michigan Department of Conservation they keep a watchful eye on the fortunes of this magnificent river system, and hovering over all of it, like two angry eagles, are two of the most remarkable men I have ever met: George Griffith of Grayling, first president and founder of Trout Unlimited, and Art Neumann of Saginaw, first vice-president. Nothing that affects the Au Sable escapes their attention. Kindly, affable, outstanding as fine hosts, both men are nevertheless fiercely protective where anything threatens the well-being of the Au Sable, and they have the solid backing of one of the largest single contingents of sophisticated trout fishermen in the United States.

There is a long list of famous Michigan names that ought to be mentioned. There is Fred Bear, transplanted Pennsylvanian from my neighborhood town of Carlisle, now a resident of Grayling, who fits in very well with the brand of hospitality dispensed by his Michigan neighbors. Fred is not only the world's most famous living archer but also a very enthusiastic trout fisherman who regards the Au Sable as one of his special concerns. On two occasions my party and I had the great pleasure of being his guests at luncheons and the rare distinction of having him as our very own guide on two fishing trips.

It was in Grayling that I met Clarence Roberts, local conservation officer and a huge man with enormous hands who, in my careful opinion, is the fastest, most accurate flytier I have ever seen. As a matter of fact, the degree of sophistication in angling techniques displayed by the Au Sable fishermen is not surpassed anywhere, except possibly in my own area in central Pennsylvania.

It is a surprising revelation to many who visit the Lower Peninsula that it is a region as rich and significant in sporting lore and history as anything in the eastern states. Anyone who is lucky enough to own or has access to two out-of-print but very significant books would better appreciate the traditional aspect of the Au Sable region. The author was William B. Mershon, pioneer conservationist and devoted sportsman who made valuable contributions to sporting literature in his two books, *The Passenger Pigeon* (1907) and *Recollections of My Fifty Years Hunting and Fishing* (1923). I am the grateful owner of both books presented to me by his son, W. B. Merson, Jr., a fine sportsman, remarkably aristocratic in bearing and speech, and worthy of his parentage.

I have painted a rather bright picture that will probably raise in the minds of many a very important question, as it did to me. How is it that anything so good as the Au Sable can exist and survive east of the Mississippi, particularly in a heavily industrialized and populous state like Michigan? To many, this must seem like an illogical oasis in the rapidly deteriorating fishing scene. The question nagged at me until I uncovered some very pertinent facts.

I have already indicated that the Au Sable river basin is a wasteland; for agricultural purposes it is one of the poorest areas in the United States. Of the basin's 1.15 million acres, only 31,000 acres are under cultivation. More importantly, the entire population of the basin was only 21,007 as of the 1960 census. The urban population does not exceed 5,500, concentrated in two small towns, Gaylord (2,568) and Grayling (2,015). The total number of people employed by a few industries amounts to 780 individuals.

It is a violent land, unattractive for permanent residence, characterized by fierce storms and deep snows with an average of 25 below-zero days in the wintertime. The best and most valuable product of this sterile land is the recreation that it provides for many thousands who go there annually. Recreational dollars are a principal source of income. It is axiomatic that the fate and treatment of any land follows the revenue line. As long as the basin continues to attract the vast array of hunters, fishermen, canoeists, skiers, and campers, it will be cared for and treated for those principal purposes. As many of us see it, the best care and treatment is simply to let it alone.

Index

Page numbers in italics refer to illustrations.

Adams fly pattern, 71-72
Au Sable River
  characteristics of, 165-69, 172, 173, 181-82
  fauna of, 168-72
  fishing in, *167*, 172-78, *174*, *175*, *179*
  noted fishermen of, 180-81

Bamboo rods, 45, 47-51, *49*, 60
Beetle fly pattern, 73
Black Spider fly pattern, 70-71
Blue Upright fly pattern, 101

Caenis (mayfly)
  fishing with, 93-103, 108-9, 114-15
  imitation, 93-94, 100-103, 105-6
  life cycle of, 91-93
  trout reaction to, 92-95
  variations of, 101
Casting
  and fly patterns, 32
  attaining skill in, 32-33
  basic principle of, 39-42
  for *Caenis* fishing, 105-6, 108-9, 110-11
  pitch in, 36, 37
Casts
  and reel weight, 40-41
  angle of, 37
  bounce (kick-back), 34-37
  curve, 34
  dragging of, 29-31, 34
  false, 36-37
  final (power), 34-35, 37
  in wind, 37
  length of, 35, 52-54, 57-58
  puddle, 35-37
  rod length and, 52-54
  wiggle, 34
Cricket fly pattern, 73-74
Crompton, Robert, 42, 54
Currents and weeds, 33-34

Curve casts, 34
Cut wings, 86

Dotterel fly pattern, 71
Drag, 29-31, 34
Drifting of trout, 8, 22, *23*, 34, 36, 111
Dry flies, construction of, 85-90
Dry-fly fishing, 80-82

Emerger, dangling, *83*, 84-85
Eyesight of fish, 9-26

Final (power) cast, 34-35, 37
Float, 32, 34-37, 111
Fly
  above and below surface film, 26, 80-85
  dragging of, 29-31, 34
  houseflies, 65-68
  placing and presentation of, 31-33
  small, "midge" fishing and, 132, 138-44
  spinner, 26, 74-78, *75*, *79*
  trout's view of, *16-17*, 22-25, 26
Fly-fishing, dynamics of, 9-26
Fly patterns, materials, and construction of, 32, 68-90, *75*, *77*, *79*, *83*, *86*, *88*
Freestone rivers, 8, 33, 152, 153, 158-64, *165*

Gold-ribbed Hare's Ear fly pattern, 83-84
Grasshoppers, 117-20, 124-31
Greenwell's Glory fly pattern, 81-83
Gut-cunning of trout, 31

Halford, Frederic, 11, 32, 69, 74, 80, 81, 84
Harris, J. R., 85
Hills, Major, 31-33, 107
Hooks, small, 138-43, *142*
Housefly, 65-68

Jassid fly pattern, 73

Kick-back (bounce) casts, 34-37

La Branche, George, 31-32, 42
Leader
    action of, 29-31, 35, 37
    for *Caenis* fishing, 95-98, 111-12
    silkworm gut, 63-64, 97-98
Leonard, Fannie, 93
Leonard, Justin, 93
Light pattern, *16-18*
Limestone, formation of, 147-49
Limestone rivers, 8, 33-34, 149-58, *151,
    155,* 159-60
Line
    Dacron backing, 41
    silk, 35, 63
    taper of, 35, 41
    weight of, 35, 41-42
Lose, Charles, 161

Male black gnat fly pattern, 69-70
Mayfly. *See* Caenis
Mershon, William B., 181
Michigan Hopper fly pattern, 126
"Midge" fishing, 132-38, *136, 139, 141,*
    143-44
Miller, Hazen L., 165, 180

Nymph, hanging, *83,* 84-85

Palmer grasshopper fly pattern, 125-26
Pitch of cast, 36, 37
Pontoon Hopper fly pattern, 127-29, *127*
Power (final) casts, 34
Puddle casts, 35-37

Red Quill fly pattern, 69
Reels, 40-41
Refraction, 16-25, 26
    laws of, 10-26, *13, 25*
Rise
    mechanics of, 5-8, 27-30
    patterns of, 106-10, *108,* 130
Rivers. *See* Freestone rivers; Limestone
    rivers
Rods
    action of, *43-46, 45,* 51, 52, 54, 56, 58

and length, importance of, 41, 42, 44,
    51-54, *53*
bamboo, 45, 47-51, *49,* 60
butt design of, *57*
convex-tapered, *55,* 55-56, *56,* 59, 60
designing of, 44-60
for *Caenis* fishing, 98, 111-12
function of, 39-42
in other materials, 47, 50-52
old-fashioned, 42-43
parabolic and progressive tapers of, 58-
    59
short, 54
stiffness of, 35, 42, 52, 54-56, 59, 98
straight-tapered, 54-55, *55, 56,* 60
Ronalds, Alfred, 11, 18

Slant tank, experiment with, *15-18*
Spinner fly, 26, 74-78, *75, 79*

Tackle for *Caenis* fishing, 98-100, 111-12
Thorax, tie style, *88,* 88-90
Trout
    brook, 161-64
    brown (mountain), 31-32
    Caenis and, 92-96, 105-11
    eyesight of, *14, 16-19,* 20-21, *21-24*
    feeding habits of, 6-8, 31-32, 65
    inspection of prey by, 7, 8, 20-21, *21,*
        27-31
    legendary, 117-24, *121*
    "midge" fishing and, 132-35, *136,* 137-
        38, *139, 141, 142,* 143-44
    mirror experiment on, *15-18*
    refraction and, *16-19, 21-25,* 26
    rise patterns of, 106-10, *108,* 130
    seasons for, 104, 124-35
    selection of prey by, 7, 8, 65
    window of, *14,* 14-26, *15-19, 21-25*
Trout Unlimited, 180

Water, surface film of, 26, 80-85
Weeds and current, 33-34
Wet-fly fishing, 80-82
Wiggle casts, 34
Window of trout, *14,* 14-26, *15-19, 21-25*
Wing-cutters, *86*
Wood, A. H. E., 98